Ethnic Knitting
Discovery

Ethnic Knitting
Discovery

The Netherlands, Denmark, Norway, and The Andes

by Donna Druchunas

NOMAD PRESS ❦ FORT COLLINS, COLORADO

Dedication

For my mother, who always encouraged me to be creative.

~~~~~~

Cover design © 2007 TLC Graphics, www.TLCGraphics.com, design by Monica Thomas

Illustrations:

Gayle Ford—Reference and technique drawings on pages 14, 18, 25, 27 (right), 28, 35, 71, and 72 copyright © 2007 by Gayle Ford.

Deborah Robson—Flat textile drawings and schematics on pages 12, 13, 27 (left), 42, 45, 48, 52, 58, 62, 76, 79, 82, 86, 92, 96, 108, 110, 112, 116, 122, 126, 144, 147, 150, 154, 160, and 164 copyright © 2007 by Deborah Robson.

Joyce M. Turley (www.dixoncovedesign.com)—Project feature and technique drawings on pages 43, 49, 59, 77, 83, 93, 105, 109, 113, 123, 135, 136, 137, 138, 139, 145, 151, and 161 copyright © 2007 by Joyce Mirhan Turley.

Front cover sweaters designed and knitted by Debbie O'Neill; back cover hat designed and knitted by Kris Paige

Cover photos by Dominic Cotignola

Interior design by Deborah Robson

Interior image processing by Rebekah Robson-May

Copyediting, proofreading, and index by Kathryn Banks, Eagle-Eye Indexing

Special thanks to Ann Budd

Books by Donna Druchunas

Ethnic Knitting Discovery *
Arctic Lace *
The Knitted Rug

* Published by Nomad Press.

Author website: www.sheeptoshawl.com

ISBN-13   978-0-9668289-3-1
ISBN-10   0-9668289-3-3

Printed in the United States of America

10 9 8 7 6 5 4 3 2 1

Nomad Press
PO Box 484
Fort Collins CO 80522–0484

www.nomad-press.com

This book is an introduction to a few of the many knitting traditions from around the world. It contains texture and color patterns from different regions and provides instructions for designing and knitting sweaters with different shapes and specific construction techniques. It is prepared with appreciation for the knitters who have come before us.

Ethnic Knitting Discovery—Drop-shoulder sweaters, with and without half-gussets and steeks, from the Netherlands, Denmark, Norway, and The Andes.

The cover sweaters are described on pages 121 (upper sweater) and 163 (lower sweater).

The fonts used to compose the charts were designed by David Xenakis, who has generously made them available for use by other knitters and designers in both amateur and professional capacities, as long as their source is credited—which we are delighted to do. This is an enormous service to the knitting community. Knitter's Symbols fonts used courtesy Knitter's Magazine—Copyright © 1998 XRX, Inc.

Nomad Press contributes a percentage of its resources to non-profit organizations working on projects related to the topics of its books.

Nomad Press proudly participates in the Green Press Initiative, which works to create paper-use transformations that conserve natural resources and preserve endangered resources.

Library of Congress Cataloging-in-Publication Data

Druchunas, Donna.
    Ethnic knitting discovery : the Netherlands, Denmark, Norway, and the Andes / by Donna Druchunas.
        p. cm.
    Summary: "Introduction to traditional knitting techniques from the Netherlands, Denmark, Norway, and the Andes, with small projects to build skills followed by drop-shoulder pullover sweaters. Techniques include color and texture patterning; simple color work; half-gussets; knitted, cut, or steeked armholes; and decorative edgings"—Provided by publisher.
    Includes bibliographical references and index.
    ISBN-13: 978-0-9668289-3-1 (alk. paper)
    ISBN-10: 0-9668289-3-3 (alk. paper)
    1. Knitting—Patterns. 2. Sweaters. I. Title.
TT825.D745 2007
746.43'2041—dc22

                                            2007006114

Contents

Introduction

Around the world, in places with different cultures, languages, and national costumes, people knit and wear sweaters that are remarkably similar in construction. With stitch patterns passed down in families and techniques learned from friends and neighbors, it is natural to find knitting skills spreading from town to town in local regions. However, as I researched this book, I was surprised to discover how often the same techniques might be used in two cities separated by a mountain range—or on two continents separated by an ocean.

But knitters have always been curious creatures, on the lookout for new techniques and design ideas. Whenever traders, sailors, and colonists traveled far from their homes, knitters met these travelers, copied the designs, and integrated the new ideas into their own knitting styles.

Although similar sweater constructions are found in many places—fishermen's sweaters were knitted in England, Ireland, and Holland, for example—techniques evolved as the sweater designs were adapted by local knitters, and sweaters were decorated with unique patterns in each region. In some areas, textured patterns were popular. In others, designs knitted with multiple colors were favored.

In past centuries, knitting was a required skill for women—and for men in a few places. Children learned to knit from their parents, and knitting was often taught in school along with reading and writing. Knitters worked without patterns, making sweaters, socks, mittens, and other items in basic shapes using techniques that had been passed down like favorite recipes. Knowing how to shape a sleeve or turn the heel of a sock was as basic as knowing how to boil water. This started to change only in the nineteenth century when many knitters started following the printed patterns published in ladies' magazines and by yarn companies.

Today, published patterns are everywhere. But that doesn't mean you can find just the right pattern when you have a project in mind. Just as having five hundred TV stations doesn't mean there's anything worth watching, having five hundred knitting books doesn't mean you can find a pattern in the right size, the right colors, and the right shape for your needs.

This book is the answer to that dilemma. With the skills you will learn in the following chapters, you will be able to design and knit beautiful, one-of-a-kind sweaters that fit perfectly.

Chapter 1 explains what you need to know to get started with ethnic knitting. If you feel intimidated by the idea of designing your own sweaters, start here for a quick boost in confidence.

Chapter 2 provides instructions for a few basic skills. If you've never knitted in the round or used knitting charts before, read over this chapter to see how easy it is!

What is ethnic knitting?

The term *ethnic knitting* describes traditional knitting techniques used in different parts of the world to create sweaters and accessories that are unique to each country or region. While differing in details, ethnic knits share a few common traits:

✧ In most cases, garments and accessories are knitted in the round using double-pointed and circular needles.

✧ There are no line-by-line instructions or written patterns.

✧ Each item is original—a unique combination of pattern stitches and colors—knitted using the traditional techniques of the region.

✧ Stitch patterns and knitting techniques are passed on to new knitters by families and friends.

Chapters 3 through 6 feature knitting techniques and designs from the Netherlands, Denmark, Norway, and the Andes. Each of these chapters includes:

✓ A small **practice project** such as a hat, headband, or purse

✓ A **general description of the sweater construction techniques** used in the region, for advanced knitters who can work from that level of abstraction

✓ **Visual sweater plans** for knitters who are ready to fill in the numbers and do the math on their own with a few clues

✓ **Sweater planning worksheets** for knitters who like to plan their own projects and figure out all of the measure-ments and stitch counts in advance

✓ **Step-by-step project sheets** for those knitters who may need to be guided through the process the first few times

I hope that the ethnic knitting techniques I present in this book free you from the need to follow patterns and give you the ability to create unique garments that reflect both historical cul-tures and your own design sensibility.

Knitting without patterns, using time-tested ethnic techniques, is often easier than following line-by-line instructions.

Freedom from patterns

Many knitters are afraid to make a single change in a pattern, and would never think of knitting a whole project without written instructions. But knitting without patterns, using time-tested ethnic knitting techniques, is often easier than following line-by-line instructions. In the following sections, I explain what you need to know and, perhaps more importantly, what you don't need to know in order to get started designing your own accessories and sweaters.

What you don't need to know

Knitter's math

We've all heard knitting nightmares about sweaters made to fit giants and pullovers where one sleeve reaches to the waist and the other dangles to the knees. We've also heard about the dreaded "knitter's math" that we are supposed to learn shortly after we master casting on and binding off.

There is no such thing as knitter's math. . . .

Let me start by assuring you that there is no such thing as knitter's math and knitting sweaters that fit is not rocket science.

Addition, subtraction, multiplication, and division are merely the 'rithmetic taught to grade-school students as part of the "3 Rs." I love math—calculus, geometry, trigonometry—but I hate arithmetic. I never properly learned my times tables, and I had the mumps when my third-grade class learned long division. In junior high school, I often failed algebra tests because I forgot that 6 × 5 = 30.

If you are like me, don't worry! Designing sweaters only requires attention to detail plus basic arithmetic skills—or a calculator. If you can figure how much change you should get at the grocery store, double a recipe, or help your third-grader with her homework, you can design your own sweaters.

Color theory

You do not need a degree in art appreciation or color theory to design your own sweaters. You choose colors every day. The paint in your kitchen, the fabric of your bedspread, the clothes in your closet are all examples of color palettes that you like. Take a look at your clothes, concentrating on the garments that you wear most often. If there's a designer outfit in the back corner of the closet collecting dust, leave it there. The clothes you are most comfortable in reveal your true style. Note the colors that are most common.

For more inspiration, go to the library or bookstore and thumb through a few fashion and decorating magazines. Buy the ones that you like, and make a collage of the pictures that you find most attractive. Put the collage on a bulletin board to inspire you. Take it to the knitting store when you shop for yarn.

As you begin designing your own projects, start with the small accessories at the beginnings of chapters 3 through 6. I designed accessories for a year before I designed my first sweater.

If you are new to designing your own projects, start with the small accessories at the beginnings of the chapters.

Knit it your way

In this book I provide three different approaches to designing knitwear.

Option 1 is the method that I prefer—using *as few calculations as possible and making things up as you go.* For knitters who enjoy this approach, I've provided a visual plan that you can use to note measurements, gauge, and stitch counts as you work on your sweater.

Option 2 is for the perfectionists among us—those who like to use *precise calculations and plan a whole sweater in advance.* For knitters who prefer this approach, I've provided a worksheet to help you calculate all of your measurements and stitch counts before you start knitting.

Option 3 is for those who need a little extra confidence boost—or those who expect they will be interrupted frequently while knitting! It provides *a step-by-step guide* for each project to help you get your feet wet.

Coping with color

Fear of color is very common. I have a great natural sense of color and I can match buttons to a sweater without taking the yarn to the store with me. However, I am totally overwhelmed at the idea of trying to design a sweater with more than two or three colors. To overcome designer's block, try these shortcuts:

✦ Start with single-color projects that have texture stitches.

✦ Buy yarns that come in families of coordinating shades.

✦ In a two-color pattern, use a solid for your main color and select a self-striping yarn for the contrasting color.

✦ Work with hand-painted or variegated yarns with a variety of colors that have been chosen for you.

With these shortcuts, you can start designing simple projects without worrying about complex charts or choosing "colors from scratch" until you gain confidence.

Small projects let you learn how colors and textures work together. They are fast and relatively inexpensive, so you don't have to worry about wasting money on yarn for an experiment.

The key is to start where you are comfortable. Don't try to design a twenty-five-color masterpiece if you've never designed a simple pullover or even a hat.

In each section on color and texture knitting, I describe the colors that are traditionally used in garments made in the pertinent region and provide suggestions for choosing your own contemporary color schemes.

What you do need to know

To consistently knit sweaters that fit the people you are making them for, you must learn a few basics about sweater shapes, silhouettes, and sizes. And you must *always* knit a gauge swatch.

The most basic sweater shapes

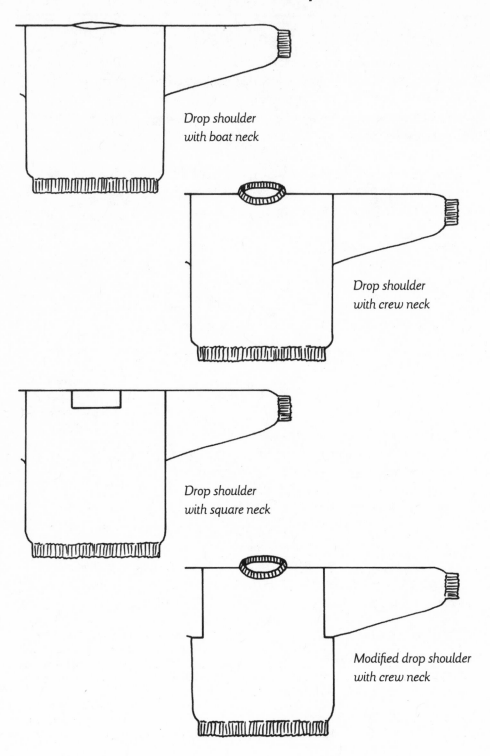

Drop shoulder
with boat neck

Drop shoulder
with crew neck

Drop shoulder
with square neck

Modified drop shoulder
with crew neck

Simple sweater shapes

Sweaters are all very similar in their basic shape—they consist of one long tube that encases the body plus two smaller tubes that extend outward from the shoulders to encase the arms. Add a hole in the top for the head to pop out and—presto!—you have a sweater. The different construction techniques that can be used to knit these tubular garments result in sweaters that have different characteristics and that will drape differently when worn by children, women, or men.

In this book I present the most basic sweater shapes, those that are made with little or no shaping, so you can concentrate on learning basic sweater construction as well as the color and texture techniques.

You'll be able to design sweaters to any size and silhouette you choose. That's the point of this approach to knitting!

Simple sweater proportions

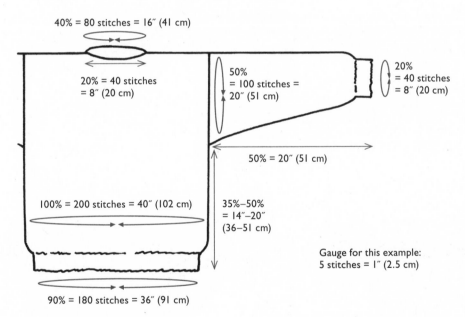

40% = 80 stitches = 16″ (41 cm)

20% = 40 stitches = 8″ (20 cm)

50% = 100 stitches = 20″ (51 cm)

20% = 40 stitches = 8″ (20 cm)

50% = 20″ (51 cm)

100% = 200 stitches = 40″ (102 cm)

35%–50% = 14″–20″ (36–51 cm)

Gauge for this example: 5 stitches = 1″ (2.5 cm)

90% = 180 stitches = 36″ (91 cm)

My preliminary work for this book was based on ideas presented by Meg Swansen and Priscilla Gibson-Roberts (see bibliography on page 170). If you know about EPS (Elizabeth's Percentage System), you're aware that Elizabeth Zimmermann introduced this way of thinking about sweaters to many contemporary knitters, although I haven't (yet) read her books.

The proportions above are based on Priscilla Gibson-Roberts' *Knitting in the Old Way*. I've simplified even further, generally dividing the body circumference by 2, 3, 4, or 5 instead of working with percentages.

As you become familiar with this style of knitting, you can refine the proportions and methods to suit your own preferences.

Sweater silhouettes

Each sweater shape can be knitted to different dimensions, creating a unique silhouette.

Silhouette is determined by two factors: ease and length. The ease of a sweater determines how snugly it fits your body. The length of a sweater determines where the hem of the sweater hits your body when you wear it.

Ease and length normally come together in a few classic combinations, but fashion designers often play with these two factors to create trendy (even outlandish) runway styles. In general, shorter sweaters are designed to fit more snugly than longer sweaters.

Tunics are usually oversized or loose fitting, intended to be worn over slender slacks or leggings. They may be slightly longer than hip length or long enough to reach mid thigh.

Measurements on the body

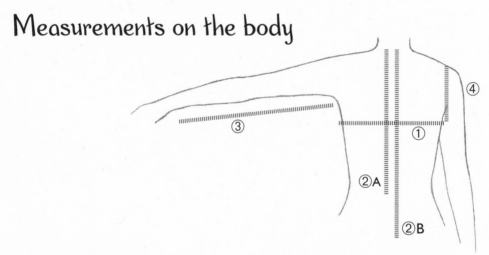

① Chest/bust: Measure around the fullest part of the chest/bust. Do not draw the tape too tightly.

② A—Back length to waist: Measure from the most prominent bone at base of neck to the natural waistline. B—Back length to hip: Measure from the same prominent bone at the base of the neck to the high hip.

③ Sleeve length to underarm: With arm slightly bent, measure from armpit to cuff.

Tip: Sleeve length to underarm is often very similar to back waist length.

④ Armhole depth: This is a guesswork measurement from the tip of the shoulder to a point about even with where you take the chest/bust measurement.

Adapted from www.yarnstandards.com/sizing.html.

Waist- and hip-length sweaters have enough ease to allow you to move freely, but not so much that you seem to be swimming in the sweater. These garments are very flexible. They go well with skirts, jeans, and slacks, and can even be worn over simple dresses.

Cropped tops and tanks are usually body hugging, to be worn with jeans, shorts, or tight skirts. Some cropped cardigans also look pretty over dresses.

If you examine your favorite sweaters and compare them to the diagrams of sweater shapes that follow, you will probably find that the sweaters you like the best have similar silhouettes.

Ease

Desired fit	Sweater measurement at chest/bust (adjust from body chest/bust measurement)
Very close fit	Actual chest/bust measurement or less
Close fit	+ 1–2″ (2.5–5 cm)
Standard fit	+ 2–4″ (5–10 cm)
Loose fit	+ 4–6″ (10–15 cm)
Oversized	+ 6″ or more (15 cm or more)

Note: You'll see there's some overlap in the amounts of ease. For example, 2″ (5 cm) can result in either standard or close fit, or 4″ (10 cm) can result in either loose or standard fit. Smaller sizes need less ease than larger sizes to achieve the more generous fit designations. Thicker yarns generally need more ease as well because the yarn bulk itself takes up some of what would be ease room.

I prefer to measure one of my favorite sweaters or sweatshirts and copy its dimensions, rather than work from a size chart, but charts become very useful when I design sweaters for other people. The set of charts on page 16 comes from the Craft Yarn Council of America's *Standards and Guidelines for Crochet and Knitting*. They provide basic information for estimating ease and length. The charts list the dimensions of basic sizes for children, women, and men. The drawing on page 13 shows the relative proportions of a sweater.

Length

Sizes	Waist length	Hip length	Tunic length
Children	Actual body measurement to waist	2″ (5 cm) below waist	6″ (15 cm) below waist
Women	Actual body measurement to waist	6″ (15 cm) below waist	11″ (28 cm) below waist
Men	Men's length usually varies only 1–2″ (2.5–5 cm) from the actual "back length to hip" measurement, as noted at 2B on the illustration opposite. Pick a length that is likely to look good on the person you are measuring.		

Standard sizes

Children

Size		4	6	8	10	12	14
Chest	inches	23	25	26½	28	30	31½
	cm	58.5	63.5	67.5	71	76	80
Back waist to neck	inches	9½	10½	12½	14	15	15½
	cm	24	26.5	32	35.5	38	39.5
Sleeve length to underarm	inches	10½	11½	12½	13½	15	16
	cm	26.5	29	32	34.5	38	40.5

Women

Size		XS	S	M	L	XL	XXL
Bust	inches	28–30	32–34	36–38	40–42	44–46	48–50
	cm	71–76	81–86	91.5–96.5	101.5–106.5	112–117	122–127
Back waist to neck	inches	16½	17	17¼	17½	17¾	18
	cm	42	43	44	44.5	45	45.5
Sleeve length to underarm	inches	16½	17	17	17½	17½	18
	cm	42	43	43	44.5	44.5	45.5

Men

Size		S	M	L	XL	XXL
Chest	inches	34–36	38–40	42–44	46–48	50–52
	cm	86–91.5	96.5–101.5	106.5–112	117–122	127–132
Back waist to neck	inches	25	26½	27	27½	28½
	cm	63.5	67.5	68.5	70	72.5
Sleeve length to underarm	inches	18	18½	19½	20	20½
	cm	45.5	47	49.5	51	52

Adapted, with minor modifications, from www.yarnstandards.com, compiled by Craft Yarn Council of America.

Gauge and swatching

The most important factor in knitting a sweater that fits is figuring out how many stitches you need. To do that, you must have an accurate gauge swatch.

If you're a swatch-resister, don't groan. Knitting a gauge swatch can be fun. It gives you the chance to try new yarns, play with colors, and learn the stitch patterns you've chosen for your project. That way you avoid making mistakes in the actual sweater. If you save all your swatches, you can eventually sew them together into a lap blanket, an afghan, or a tote bag. Or you can keep your swatches in a knitter's journal with a yarn label, your knitting notes, and a photo of your finished project.

The sample sweaters

I've chosen simple numbers to display the calculations for the examples in this book. All of them are based on a gauge of 5 stitches to 1 inch (the equivalent of 20 stitches to 10 cm).

Most of the examples show how to construct a 40-inch (102-cm) sweater, because at 5 stitches to the inch that size results in a nice, neat 200 stitches for the main number of stitches. This makes it easy to see what I am doing with the calculations. Because of differences in ease (see page 15), the same 40-inch sweater will relate as follows to people with the chest/bust measurements noted:

  40-inch: very close fit

  38–39-inch: close fit

  36–38-inch: standard fit

  34–36-inch: loose fit

  34-inch or smaller: oversized

Of course, you'll be able to design sweaters to any size and silhouette you choose. That's the point of this approach to knitting!

A swatch is a gift to yourself that keeps on giving!

Making a gauge swatch is easy. Using the same stitch pattern you will use in your project and needles that are an appropriate size for the yarn you've chosen (see page 22), cast on 20 to 24 stitches, and work until you have about 5 inches (12.5 cm) of knitting. If your project will be knitted in the round, your swatch should also be knitted in the round. Many knitters find that they get a different gauge on the same pattern when knitting circularly than they do when knitting back and forth.

If you don't relish swatching a small number of stitches on double-pointed needles, here's a trick that will let you knit your "in the round" swatch flat on a circular needle. Don't turn at the end of the row. Slide the stitches to the other end of the circular needle, loosely strand the yarn across the back of the work, and continue with the next row.

Measuring stitch gauge

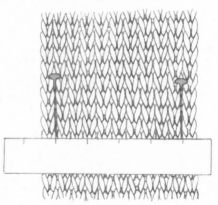

How to measure gauge

Stitch gauge is important in almost all projects. If your stitch gauge is not exact, your sweater will not come out the right size. To measure the stitch gauge, place a ruler or tape measure across your swatch horizontally. Mark the beginning and end of 4 inches (10 cm) with pins. Count the stitches between the pins. A half or quarter stitch does matter.

Measuring row gauge

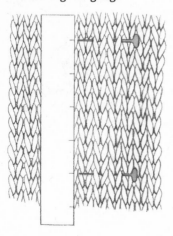

Row gauge is less important because on most projects you can knit to the desired length without counting rows. However, row gauge can be important when you knit color or texture patterns that form pictures, or if you want to place a particular pattern within a given area. If your rows are too short or too tall, the designs will be distorted or they won't fit. To measure the row gauge, place a ruler or tape measure across your swatch vertically. Mark the beginning and end of 4 inches (10 cm) with pins and count the rows. A half row matters, although not as much as partial stitches do for stitch gauge.

The feel and look of your fabric

Measuring stitches and rows per inch (cm) is only one reason to knit a gauge swatch. Other important reasons include:

✓ Practicing the pattern stitches you will use in your project.

✓ Testing color combinations.

✓ Deciding what needle size(s) to use.

When your swatch is finished, bind off. Take the swatch in your hand. Feel the fabric, look at the texture and the shape of the stitches, and hold the swatch up to the light to see how densely the stitches are packed. If the fabric is too dense and stiff, swatch again on a larger needle. If the fabric is limp and the stitches look sloppy, work another swatch on a smaller needle. When you re-swatch, you can try a different pattern stitch or color combination if you didn't care for the choices you made the first time. Tie knots in the tail of yarn attached to each swatch, using a code that you devise to help you remember what size needle you used.

After you make a gauge swatch that pleases you, you're ready to start filling in the sweater-planning worksheets for your project.

Ready to move on? Chapter 2 explains a few basic knitting techniques to help you get started.

Knitting a gauge swatch gives you a chance to play.

A few basics

If you've never knitted in the round before, this chapter will give you a tour of the basic techniques you'll be using in the sweaters and other projects presented in this book. Skim this information now, if you are so inclined, or refer to these pages when you need to know something specific.

Yarn and supplies

Ethnic-style knitting uses the same basic supplies as other approaches to knitting. For the most part, you use circular and double-pointed needles. You will find that certain kinds of yarns are better for specific projects. In each project, I provide yarn suggestions. The following guidelines will give you an overview of what is available in the world of needles and yarns.

Knitting needles

For ethnic knitting, you will use circular and double-pointed knitting needles more often than straight needles. Circular and double-pointed needles come in a variety of materials, and they are made in all the standard knitting-needle sizes.

Each pair of circular needles is connected by a long cable. Cables come in lengths from 11 to 60 inches (in metric, you'll find lengths from 30 to 150 cm, although an 11-inch circular is 25 cm long). For knitting sweaters, you will need a 16-inch (40-cm) needle for the sleeves and a 29- to 32-inch (70- to 80-cm) needle for the sweater body. If you already have needles close to these lengths in your toolkit, feel free to try them. These lengths are just guidelines. The key is to make sure your needle is a few inches (or a few centimeters) smaller than the circumference of the piece you will be knitting so the stitches reach comfortably around the needle.

Double-pointed needles come in sets of four or five needles. Sets of four tend to come from the United States while the sets of five tend to come from Europe. You can use either type of set; you may have a preference for one or the other. These needles are used for knitting items or sweater parts, such as cuffs, that are too small to fit on even a short circular needle.

Many knitters prefer to knit ribbings, cuffs, and neckbands on needles one or two sizes smaller than their main needle size. On many of the patterns, I've noted this as optional. Sometimes I change sizes, and sometimes I don't.

Needle sizes

U.S. needle size	Metric needle size
1	2.25 mm
2	2.75 mm
3	3.25 mm
4	3.5 mm
5	3.75 mm
6	4 mm
7	4.5 mm
8	5 mm
9	5.5 mm
10	6 mm
10½	6.5 mm
11	8 mm
13	9 mm
15	10 mm

The manufacturers' metric and imperial specifications for knitting needles don't correspond exactly with each other. Don't worry about it. Pick something in the right range, cast on, and start swatching.

Source: www.yarnstandards.com, Craft Yarn Council of America.

Yarn

There are so many different types of yarn that many people find it intimidating to select the best yarn for a project. Yarns fall into three general fiber categories—animal fiber, plant fiber, and man-made. Each category has different properties, and knowing what those properties are can help you select working materials that are appropriate for your needs.

Wool yarns are my favorites, followed by yarns made from other animal fibers like alpaca, cashmere, and mohair. Many of these yarns have a lot of give and are easy on the hands. Most are also well suited to ethnic-style knitting because they have a texture that allows the knitting to hold together well. When you have knitted with wool and you cut an armhole or neckline opening, you won't have to worry about the knitting falling apart. I think that every knitter should experience the pleasure of knitting with animal fibers on wooden or bamboo needles. However, many experienced knitters enjoy knitting wool with slick metal needles, which allow the work to go very quickly.

While you are learning this process, focus on yarn weights 2 through 5. Extra light or heavy yarns require minor adjustments that you will know how to make once you have experience.

Yarn guidelines

Yarn weight	1	2	3	4	5	6
Type of yarn	Sock, fingering, or baby	Sport, baby	DK, light worsted	Worsted, Aran	Chunky	Bulky
Gauge range: stitches in 4 inches (10 cm) in stockinette stitch	27–32	23–26	21–24	16–20	12–15	6–11
Suggested U.S. needle size	1–3	3–5	5–7	7–9	9–11	11 or larger
Suggested metric needle side	2.25–3.25 mm	3.25–3.75 mm	3.75–4.5 mm	4.5–5.5 mm	5.5–8 mm	8 mm or larger

All specifications here are suggested starting points for determining appropriate gauges and needle sizes. Your own gauge swatch will be your true guide. Information on this page adapted from www.yarnstandards.com, Craft Yarn Council of America.

Cotton and other plant fibers are very comfortable, especially for those who live in warm climates. Yarns made from these fibers do not have the same give that yarns made from animal fibers have. They are also sometimes quite slippery, which can make them more difficult to work with. Wooden or bamboo needles are best for these fibers because the needles' texture makes it less likely that you will drop stitches. Because plant fibers are often slick, they are not as easy to work with when you want to cut an armhole or neck opening. Although you can cut openings in knitted cotton fabric, after machine stitching the parts that will be cut, I suggest that you use cotton yarns in projects that don't require cutting until you get some practice with making cut openings in wool fabrics.

Acrylics, other man-made fibers, and blends can be used in all of the projects in this book. Yarns made from these fibers are often economical and can wear well. I still regularly wear acrylic sweaters that my grandmother made more than fifty years ago. They go in the washer and dryer, and they still look brand-new. Man-made

Approximate yarn quantities

Child's sweater
Chest 26–34″ (66–86 cm)

Lightweight yarn	1000–1800 yards	900–1700 meters
Medium-weight yarn	900–1200 yards	850–1100 meters
Heavy-weight yarn	700–1000 yards	650-900 meters

Woman's hip-length sweater
Bust 32–44″ (81–112 cm)

Lightweight yarn	1500–2600 yards	1400–2400 meters
Medium-weight yarn	1100–1700 yards	1000–1600 meters
Heavy-weight yarn	1000–1100 yards	900–1000 meters

Man's hip-length sweater
Chest 36–50″ (91–127 cm)

Lightweight yarn	1800–3000 yards	1700–2750 meters
Medium-weight yarn	1500–2000 yards	1400–1850 meters
Heavy-weight yarn	1300–1500 yards	1200–1400 meters

These yarn estimates are for sweaters knitted in one color in stockinette stitch or a lightly textured pattern.

Sources: Modified from Vicki Square, *The Knitter's Companion,* and Ann Budd, *The Knitter's Handy Guide to Yarn Requirements.*

fibers are not as breathable as natural fibers, which means they may not be as comfortable to wear in certain climates or seasons.

The yarn estimates in the chart on page 23 are for sweaters knitted in one color in stockinette stitch or a lightly textured pattern. You will need 20 to 30 percent more yarn for a densely textured sweater. When using multiple colors, you will also need 20 to 35 percent more yarn, divided up between the colors. You will have to estimate based on how much of each color you plan to use in your design.

Always buy more yarn than you think you will need. Check with your yarn shop about its return policy. Most shops will allow you to return extra yarn for credit within one year of your purchase.

Knitting in the round

Many ethnic-style knitting projects are knitted in the round. Although the upper body portions of the Dutch and Danish sweaters in chapters 3 and 4 are knitted back and forth, in each case the main body and the sleeves are knitted in the round. The Norwegian and Andean sweaters in chapters 5 and 6 are knitted entirely in the round.

Knitting in the round is quite easy, and many people love circular knitting so much they never knit back and forth once they've tried it. Working in the round eliminates the need to sew seams, which can be an added bonus if you don't like finishing. In addition, the right side of the knitting is always visible, making it easier to follow the charts.

Casting on and joining the first round

Start by casting on. You'll need to join the stitches into a circle without twisting them. Any easy way to do this is to place the needles on a flat surface and make sure all of the stitches are lined up on the inside of the curve of the needles. With the tail and the working yarn on the righthand needle, carefully pick up the needles and knit the first couple of stitches. This completes your join.

To continue, just knit around and around and around. You can use the yarn tail to keep track of the beginning of the round (as

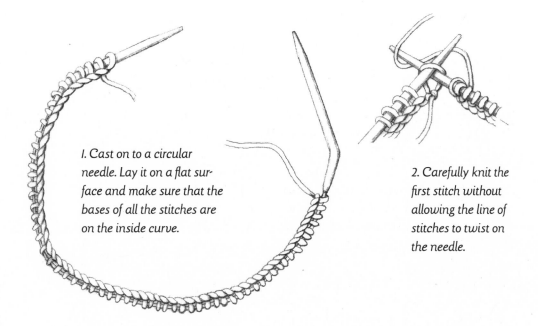

1. Cast on to a circular needle. Lay it on a flat surface and make sure that the bases of all the stitches are on the inside curve.

2. Carefully knit the first stitch without allowing the line of stitches to twist on the needle.

I do), or you can put a stitch marker onto the needle before you knit those first few stitches and slip the marker every time you come to it.

Knitting with double-pointed needles (often abbreviated *dpns*) is not very different, but some people find it slightly awkward until they get used to it, while others find it simple and natural from the start. After a while, switching needles as you progress around the circle becomes part of the rhythm of knitting.

When working on double-pointed needles, cast onto one needle—you may want to cast onto a circular needle—and then divide the stitches evenly on either three or four needles. Do this by just slipping groups of stitches from the cast-on needle to the other needles. You can put your work on three needles and knit with the fourth (my preference, and common in the United States), or you can put your work on four needles and knit with the fifth (common in Europe). If you've never used double-pointed needles before, try both setups to see which is most comfortable for you.

To start the first round on double-pointed needles, make sure the bases of the stitches are lined up on the inside of the triangle (or square) formed by the needles. Carefully knit the first stitch.

Again, joining the first round into a circle is the trickiest part of working this way. Place the needles on a flat surface and make sure the bases of all the stitches are lined up on the inside of the triangle or square formed by the needles. With the tail and the working yarn on the righthand needle, carefully pick up the needles and knit the first couple of stitches. This joins the knitting so you are ready to work in the round.

Getting used to circular knitting

If you are new to knitting in the round, I suggest you try a small project first. A hat is a good choice, because although you knit most of the hat on a circular needle you have to switch to double-pointed needles (dpns) when you knit the crown. In this case, you already have the rest of the hat knitted so switching from the circular needle to double-pointed needles is easy, and you only have to knit a few rows on the multiple needles before you are finished. When you are ready to switch from the circular needle to the double-pointed needles, pick up one double-pointed needle and knit one-fourth to one-third of the stitches onto it (one-fourth if you are working with five double-pointed needles and one-third if you are working with four). Pick up another needle and knit the second batch. Continue until you have knitted all of the stitches onto either three or four needles and you have completed the round. You will have one needle left over.

To start the next round, take the empty needle and use it to knit all of the stitches off the first needle. That first needle is now empty. Use it to knit the stitches off the second needle. Keep going in this manner, always using the just-freed needle to knit the next batch of stitches.

Cutting open armholes and necks

When you knit an entire sweater in the round, the body is one big tube. To create openings for the armholes, and sometimes for the front of the neck, you cut the knitting. Yes, you cut it with scissors.

Just cutting

The simplest type of armhole and neck openings are made with no special consideration during knitting. When your body tube is complete, simply (1) work 2 rows of machine stitching on either side of the column of stitches you plan to cut open, and also reinforce the bottom of the column by sewing back and forth a few times. Then (2) cut right down the center of the stitch column with very sharp sewing shears. You may cover the cut edge with a facing that is attached to the top of the sleeve, or you may fold the edge to the inside and stitch it down.

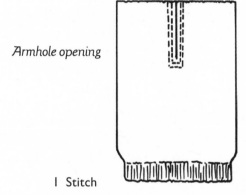

Armhole opening

I Stitch   2 Cut

To cut a neck opening, (1) sew 2 rows of machine stitching to mark the neck shaping, and then (2) cut off the excess fabric. You may enclose the cut edge in a neckband, or you may fold it to the inside and stitch it down.

Neck opening

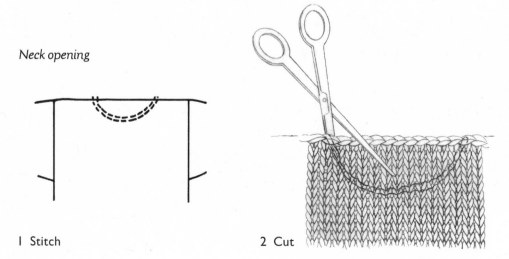

I Stitch   2 Cut

27

Steeking and cutting

You can create more complex armhole and neck openings by knitting steeks. A steek consists of a set of special stitches that can be added at the place where an armhole or neck opening will be cut. There are several ways to work a steek. Here's the one that I find easiest and most flexible.

To create a steek, either bind off or place on a holder a number of stitches where you want the armhole or neck opening to begin. The number of stitches to use for the steek varies depending on the shape of the armhole or neck opening.

Armhole steek

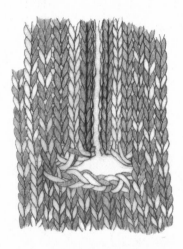

At the base of the armhole, bind off several stitches (say 7). On the next round, cast on several stitches (7 in the example).

Machine stitch on either side of the column that you plan to cut. Cut between the stitching with very sharp scissors.

The steek is inside the box. When you are doing color work, knit the steek stitches in alternating colors. You can work stripes or a checkerboard.

On the next round, cast on 3 to 7 stitches above the bound-off or reserved stitches. If you are a beginner, start with seven stitches. When you have more experience, you may want to make a smaller steek.

As you continue on the following rows, knit the steek stitches in stockinette stitch. If you are working with more than one color, knit the steek stitches in a simple, alternating color pattern.

When you are finished knitting the sweater body, machine stitch on either side of the column of stitches that you will cut, then slice the column open neatly with sharp sewing shears. Fold the steek back and sew it into place as a facing.

One major advantage to this type of armhole or neck treatment is that you can shape the armhole or neck opening by working decreases just outside the steek stitches.

Working from charts

In ethnic-style knitting, pattern stitches are usually shown in charts. In the past, knitters didn't use written patterns and they copied stitch patterns from other garments they saw their neighbors wearing. Many stories have been told about women who missed whole sermons in church because they were busy analyzing intricate cable or color patterns on the sweater of a person in the pew in front of them. Working with charts is like that, without the guesswork.

A chart is simply a picture of the stitch pattern. It is made using special symbols (for pattern stitches) or squares of colors (for color work). Each square in a chart represents one stitch. The symbols are a shorthand for the stitch, or stitch combination, to be worked. The chart symbols that I use in this book are noted below.

Symbols used in knit-and-purl charts

Symbol	Worked in the round	Worked back and forth
□	knit	knit on right side purl on wrong side
⊟	purl	purl on right side knit on wrong side

Symbols used in color charts

Symbol	
□	MC = main color
⊡	CC = contrasting color

Complex pattern stitches are much easier to knit from charts than from line-by-line instructions, because the chart provides a visual representation of what your knitting will look like. Simple pattern stitches are sometimes explained in text, but these designs can also be charted, and even they are easier to understand in visual form.

The way you go about reading a chart depends on whether you are knitting in the round or back and forth in rows, so pay careful attention if you are working on a sweater that requires you to knit part of your sweater in the round (like the lower body) and part of it back and forth (like the upper front and back sections).

To read a chart, start at the bottom for row 1 and move up the chart one row for each row or round of knitting.

☆ When working *in the round*, read every chart row from right to left.

☆ When working *back and forth*, read right-side chart rows from right to left and wrong-side chart rows from left to right. Normally the odd-numbered rows are right-side rows and the even-numbered rows are wrong-side rows. Take note that some symbols have different meanings on wrong-side rows.

It is more difficult to work the wrong-side rows because you will be looking at the back of the pattern as you knit, so on these rows you will have to pay extra attention to counting stitches. I also find it helpful to peek over the top of my knitting needles at the front of my knitting as I work across wrong-side rows. I hate ripping, and I prefer to catch my mistakes as quickly as possible.

As you knit from the charts, place a sticky note above the line you are working on. That way you can see the row you are knitting and the rows below it—which is what you will see in your fabric. Compare this to your knitting frequently. After a while, you will learn to read your knitting directly and you may find that you don't have to refer to the charts very often, especially on simple pattern stitches.

Texture: Chart and knitted sample

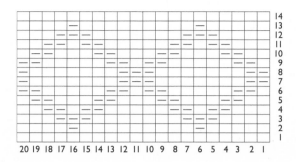

Color: Chart and knitted sample

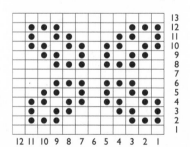

Tip: You can see by comparing the texture and color swatches that row gauge is different for different types of knitting. In the color sample, the stitches are closer to "square" than they are in the texture sample.

Centering patterns

When you work with color and texture patterns, you may want to center the designs on the body or sleeves of your sweater. Some patterns, such as a small check or an arrow design, will look fine without centering, while others, such as a large snow-flake design, may call out to be centered on your sweater. It's your choice whether to center or not.

Centering a single motif

When you are working with a single motif on the front of a sweater, you need to arrange the motif so it falls in the center of the front. This requires a few simple calculations. Fill in the blanks in the chart below with the numbers that correspond to your gauge and measurements.

Centering a motif

	Number or calculation	Example	Description
Front stitches	___	100	Begin with the **number of stitches on the front** of your sweater (half of the total number of stitches in a round).
Motif stitches	___	36	Note the **number of stitches in the motif** you have chosen
Leftover stitches	___ − ___ = ___	100 − 36 = **64**	**Subtract** the number of stitches in your motif from the number of stitches for the front.
Centering stitches	___ ÷ 2 = ___	64 ÷ 2 = **32**	Divide the result in half to calculate how to **center the motif.** This is the number of stitches on each side of the motif. *Note:* If the number of stitches in the motif is an odd number, decrease 1 stitch on a plain row before you begin to work the motif.

To begin the motif, work ___ centering stitches, place a marker, work the motif chart, place a marker, then work ___ centering stitches. Continue to work the entire motif chart be-tween the two markers, with plain stitches outside the markers.

Horizontal and all-over patterns

When you work with horizontal and all-over stitch patterns, you may want to arrange the pattern so the design is centered on both the front and back of your sweater. Centering the patterns takes a bit of thought and calculation. Fill in the blanks in the chart below with the numbers that correspond to your gauge and measurements.

Centering a horizontal or all-over pattern

	Number or calculation	Example	Description
Front stitches	____	128	Begin with the **number of stitches on the front** of your sweater (half of the total number of stitches in a round).
Pattern stitches	____	12	Note the **number of stitches in the pattern** you have chosen.
Repeats	___ ÷ ___ = ___	128 ÷ 12 = 10.8 = **10**	**Divide** the number of stitches in the front by the number of stitches in your pattern to find out how many **full pattern repeats** will fit in your stitch count. Round down.
	___ x ___ = ___	10 x 12 = **120**	**Multiply** the number of full pattern repeats by the number of stitches in each repeat.
Leftover stitches	___ − ___ = ___	128 − 120 = **8**	**Subtract** the number of stitches in your pattern repeats from the number of stitches for the front.
Centering stitches	___ ÷ 2 = ___	8 ÷ 2 = **4**	Divide the result in half to calculate how to **center the pattern.** Note: If the main number of stitches in the pattern is an odd number, decrease 1 stitch on a plain row before you begin to work the motif.

To begin the pattern, *work the last ____ stitches (number of centering stitches) of the chart, place a marker, work the required number of pattern repeats, place a marker, then work the first ____ stitches (number of centering stitches) of the chart.* (If you are centering your patterns on the front and back of a sweater body, you will repeat from * to * for the front and then for the back.) Continue to work all rows of the chart, slipping all markers as you come to them.

Some patterns have one or more extra stitches on one edge that allows the pattern to seamlessly flow around a piece of circular knitting. To center this type of chart, you may want to duplicate this column of stitches on the other end of the chart. For example, in the following chart, the pattern has a thin stripe on the right edge and in between each pair of pattern repeats. If you are centering this pattern on the top of a sweater between the armholes, you may want to add a thin stripe to the left edge as well.

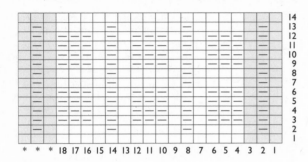

To center this pattern, stitches 1 through 3 on the right side of this chart are duplicated on the left in the three columns marked with asterisks.

If you are working on a sleeve, centering patterns can seem complicated because the number of stitches in the sleeve changes frequently. Begin by centering a pattern at the shoulder (if you're knitting the sleeve from the top down) or above the cuff (if you're knitting the sleeve from the cuff to the top). If you are increasing, work the increases into the pattern. If you are decreasing, there's nothing to fret about; the extra stitches just go away. Just watch to make sure your pattern continues to look right as you work succeeding rows or rounds.

Adjusting stitch counts for horizontal patterns

You can also adjust the number of stitches in your body to accommodate the multiple used in each pattern. If you only adjust a few stitches, it won't be noticeable. Do this in a plain row of knitting between panels.

For example, if you are working with a chart that has a 12-stitch repeat, you need a total number of stitches that is a multiple of 12 such as 216, 240, or 264. If you are working with 216 stitches and your next pattern has a multiple of 10 stitches, you need to have 220 stitches to fit the new pattern in evenly. So you would increase 4 stitches on a plain row before you start the new pattern. If you had 264 stitches, you would need to decrease 4 stitches to 260. If you had 240 stitches, you would not have to increase or decrease because 240 is evenly divisible by both 12 and 10.

If you are working on a sleeve, where the stitch count changes frequently, don't worry about having the right number of stitches. Just work the patterns into the increases as best you can.

Three-needle bind-off

The three-needle bind-off lets you join two pieces of knitting, often the shoulders of a sweater, by binding them off together. Both pieces must have the same number of stitches. If you join the pieces while holding the wrong sides together, the seam creates a decorative ridge. If you join the pieces while holding the right sides together, the seam creates a straight line.

1. Holding the two pieces together on two needles, insert a third needle into the first stitch on the front needle (as if to knit) and into the first stitch on the back needle (also as if to knit). Knit these 2 stitches together, making 1 stitch.

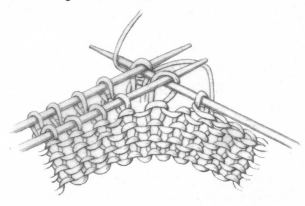

2. Knit another stitch as in step 1. You now have 2 stitches on the right needle.

3. Insert the left needle into the first stitch that you worked onto the right needle and pass it over the second stitch that you worked, dropping the first stitch off the needle— this is like a normal bind-off. One stitch remains on the right needle.

Repeat steps 2 and 3 to bind off the rest of the stitches.

Congratulations! That's all you need to know to get started with ethnic-style knitting!

The Netherlands

Some very simple textured sweater designs come from the Netherlands. Beginning in the middle of the nineteenth century, fishermen living in coastal villages began wearing sweaters decorated with knit-and-purl stitch patterns, supplemented with occasional cables. Sweaters were designed with either vertical or horizontal arrangements of pattern stitches. Frugal knitters often decorated only the top portions of sweaters, because knitting textured stitches uses more yarn and takes more time than knitting plain stockinette stitch. Some sweaters were almost entirely stockinette stitch, with a single motif decorating the center front. While the basic sweater construction was the same throughout the region, the combination of stitch patterns used by knitters in each village was unique.

Dutch fishermen's sweaters have a basic, effective shape that requires little arithmetic to design. These sweaters are knitted in a way that requires no seams whatsoever.

In a sweater of traditional proportions, the armhole measures one-third of the total length and the neck opening measures one-third of the total width. The sweater is knitted in the round to the armholes. Then the work is divided for front and back. The knitter works back and forth to complete the upper back, taking the fabric straight up from the armhole to the desired length with no shaping at all. Then the upper front is knitted in the same way until it is 2 inches (5 cm) shorter than the back. The center one-third of the front stitches are placed on hold for the neck, and each shoulder is knitted separately until the length of the front matches that of the back. The knitter joins the shoulders by binding off each set of front stitches together with its matching set of back stitches. Then stitches are picked up around the armhole and the sleeves are knitted in the round from the shoulder to the cuff. The neck shaping is accomplished by adding a ribbed neckband after the rest of the knitting has been completed. The

Dutch fishermen's sweaters have a basic, effective shape that requires little arithmetic to design.

neckline often features a drawstring decorated with pompoms.

Traditionally, Dutch fishermen's sweaters were knitted using yarn spun from the wool of local sheep. The fiber was spun tightly, to form a dense and durable yarn. The most common colors were a neutral beige and a rich shade of blue speckled with a few red fibers, called Nassau blue. The color was named for the Dutch royal family, so although it is a dark tweed, it is literally "royal blue."

These sweaters were historically made to fit snugly, perhaps as a safety precaution so the men wouldn't catch loose fabric on equipment while they worked on fishing boats and docks. For a more comfortable and contemporary silhouette, I prefer to knit this style with a softer yarn and a looser fit. As you plan your own sweater, you can choose the yarn style and dimensions that you prefer.

Chapter
3

CHAPTER HIGHLIGHTS

Skills

✓ Knit-and-purl texture patterning worked both in the round and back and forth

Techniques

✓ Centering a single motif

✓ Centering horizontal patterns

Garment styling

✓ Drop shoulder, standard pullover style

✓ Upper body sections worked back and forth

✓ Sleeves picked up at armholes and knitted down to ribbed cuffs

Pattern stitches

With only the two basic stitches in knitting—the *knit* and the *purl*—you can form an endless number of combinations. The design possibilities range from simple lines or diamonds to detailed pictures drawn with purl stitches on a stockinette-stitch background.

Garter stitch or garter ridge ↦

Worked over any number of stitches.
   Technical note: The chart shows the horizontal ridges formed by working garter stitch. Each sequence of 2 rounds or 2 rows produces 1 ridge. A set of 6 rounds or rows creates 3 ridges.

Repeat: 1 stitch by 2 rows

Worked in the round
Round 1: Knit.
Round 2: Purl.
Repeat rounds 1 and 2 for pattern.

Worked back and forth
All rows: Knit.

Seed stitch ↦

Worked over an even number of stitches.
   Technical note: While the instructions for circular and flat knitting seem to contradict each other, the chart clearly shows that you alternate knits and purls—or "purl the knits and knit the purls"—on each row or round in either method.

Repeat: 2 stitches by 2 rows

Worked in the round
Round 1: *K1, p1. Repeat from * to end of round.
Round 2: *P1, k1. Repeat from * to end of round.
Repeat rounds 1 and 2 for pattern.

Worked back and forth
All rows: *K1, p1. Repeat from * to end of row.

Anchor motif

The anchor motif is 19 stitches wide. The chart is shown with a 23-stitch width as a reminder that the figure needs to be set off by stockinette stitch on all sides (including above and below the motif).

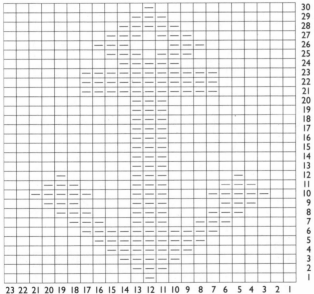

23 22 21 20 19 18 17 16 15 14 13 12 11 10 9 8 7 6 5 4 3 2 1

Motif: 19 stitches by 30 rows

Diamonds

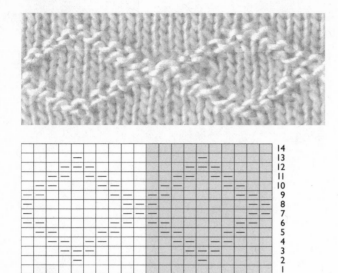

Repeat: 10 stitches (plus 1 to balance) by 14 rows

Checks

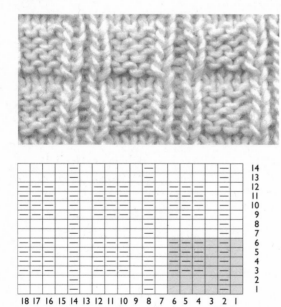

Repeat: 6 stitches (plus 3 to balance) by 6 rows (plus 2 to balance)

Arrows

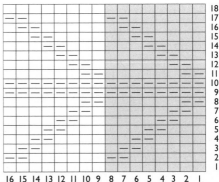

Repeat: 8 stitches by 18 rows

There was an old woman who lived in a mill. . . .

The November 1930 issue of *Needlecraft Magazine* recalls a poem about an old Dutch woman who lived in a windmill near the shore of the Zuyder Zee. She knitted so much that her windmill home filled up with scarves, mittens, hats, and mufflers. When finally there was no more room left for living, she ripped everything out and started again!

According to the 1930 article, women in Holland at the time had no choice but to knit. Machine-made garments of the time could not provide the warmth needed in their cold and damp land. Nothing could match the comfort of hand-knitted socks inside the classic wooden shoes. And during the winter, when the frozen canals became the main roads in small villages, people wore wooden ice skates that strapped directly onto their feet, with no shoes to add insulation. Warm woolen socks kept frostbite at bay!

Seaman's Scarf

Seamen's scarves fit well with the nautical theme that we are following in our exploration of Dutch knitting. Although this type of scarf did not originate in the Netherlands, it's been knitted there for more than a hundred years! The ends of a seaman's scarf are traditionally knitted in garter stitch, but they can also be decorated with pattern stitches as I'm showing here. The center of the scarf is worked in ribbing so that it fits snugly around the neck.

I borrowed this pattern concept because I wanted to offer a project that would give you a chance to practice following charts and working the pattern stitches flat. (To practice working similar stitches in the round, with the right side of the work always facing you, check out the cap pattern on page 76.)

The Dutch-inspired sweaters in this chapter require you to work knit-and-purl stitch patterns both in the round and back and forth. The lower bodies and the sleeves are worked in the round. The upper body sections, both front and back, are worked back and forth.

← Ribbing (1x1 or 2x2)

Garter stitch at ends and separating all pattern bands

← Seed stitch

← Arrows

← Diamonds

⬦ Texture stitches worked back and forth

This illustrations here and opposite show a scarf at a gauge of 5 stitches and 7 rows per inch (2.5 cm) that is 8 inches (20.5 cm) wide and has 18-inch (45.7-cm) ends.

Get ready   *yarn & needles*

Smooth yarn will show off texture patterns best. For a wind-resistant scarf, choose a tightly spun yarn and knit at a gauge that is fairly dense without producing a fabric that feels board-like. For a softer scarf, select a loosely spun yarn and knit at a gauge that produces a fabric that feels cushy, not floppy.

Any weight of yarn will work, but for practice I suggest a medium-weight yarn and U.S. size 7 or 8 (4.5 or 5 mm) knitting needles.

Approximately 400 yards (365 m) of worsted-weight wool will make a nice-sized scarf.

Needle guidelines are on page 22.

43

Get set *stitches, gauge & size*

Stitches and gauge

① Select the stitches for your scarf. Use the combination shown on the sample scarf illustration (page 42), or choose your own combination of knit-and-purl pattern stitches.

② Make a gauge swatch in each of the pattern stitches you have chosen.

Even though gauge is not critical for a scarf, it is a good idea to practice each combination to learn the pattern and to make sure you enjoy knitting it. That way you'll make any mistakes on your practice swatch instead of on your scarf. You can also decide whether you like the fabric you are producing. Sometimes a change in needle size, either up or down, can make a big difference in your satisfaction.

③ Measure your stitch gauge. Each knit-and-purl pattern stitch will work up to a slightly different gauge, but the different gauges will all be close enough to each other so that you can measure the gauge of any swatch, or measure all of your swatches and take the average. Write the stitch gauge on the planning worksheet on page 46. The row gauge can also be useful if you want to determine exact placement of your patterns within the scarf ends, but I recommend just winging it on the first end and then reversing the same patterns for the second end.

Size

① Determine how wide and long you want your scarf to be. Write the measurements on the visual plan on page 45 and the planning worksheet on page 46.

② Use the calculations on the worksheet on page 46 to figure all the remaining numbers before you start, or just calculate each new number as you need it.

③ Transfer the resulting numbers to the visual plan on page 45 or the step-by-step instructions on page 47, depending on how much guiding detail you would like to have while you knit. The visual plan can be helpful even if you are using the step-by-step project sheet as a confidence-builder.

Technical note: The edges of the scarf will undulate as you change from garter ridges to knit-and-purl pattern stitches worked on a stockinette-stitch background. I like this effect. However, if you prefer straight edges on your scarf, work a garter-stitch border along each lengthwise edge. To prepare for this, add an extra 3 or 4 stitches at the beginning and end of every row. On both right-side and wrong-side rows, knit these stitches.

Place a marker inside each set of border stitches as a reminder to switch to your pattern stitch.

Tip: Average scarves can have widths that range between 5 and 8 inches (12.5 and 20 cm), with end lengths between 10 and 15 inches (25.5 and 38 cm). You may want to make your scarf wider or narrower, and longer or shorter, for special purposes or people.

Knit!   *option I: using a visual plan*

The Netherlands
Seaman's Scarf

For knitters who are ready to work from the basic concept

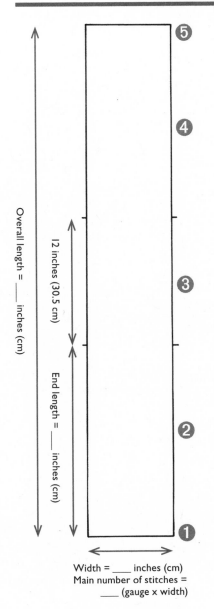

Overall length = _____ inches (cm)

12 inches (30.5 cm)

End length = _____ inches (cm)

Width = _____ inches (cm)
Main number of stitches =
_____ (gauge x width)

❶ Cast on

❷ Work first end

❸ Work center ribbed section (no shaping required; ribbing draws in naturally)

❹ Work second end

❺ Bind off

Knit!   option 2: using a planning worksheet

For knitters who want to plan thoroughly in advance

Measurements and stitch counts

	Calculation	Example	Description
Stitch gauge	____ stitches = 1 inch or 1 cm	**5** stitches = 1 inch	**Gauge** is not critical for a scarf. "Close" is good enough.
Width	____ inches (cm)	**8** inches	Desired **width** of scarf.
Total length	____ inches (cm)	**48** inches	Desired **length** of scarf.
End length	____ – 12 = ____ ____ ÷ 2 = ____	48 – 12 = **36** 36 ÷ 2 = **18**	Subtract 12 inches from the total length, and divide the result in half to calculate the **length of each end**.
Main number of stitches	____ × ____ = ____	5 × 8 = **40** stitches	Multiply the stitch gauge by the width to calculate the **main number of stitches**. See *tip*.

Need a slightly different stitch count? Increase or decrease by a few.

Tip: For some patterns, like seed stitch and ribbing, some knitters prefer to work on an odd number of stitches. I personally prefer to always work these on an even number, but if you like the other approach and you get an even number for your main number of stitches, add or subtract 1 stitch.

Knit! *option 3: a step-by-step project sheet*

The Netherlands
Seaman's Scarf

For knitters who would like detailed instructions

Do the calculations on the planning worksheet on page 46 so you have the numbers to fill in here.

❶ Cast on

Cast on **main number of stitches:** ____ stitches.

❷ Work first end

*Work 3 garter ridges (6 rows).

Work a full repeat of the texture pattern stitch of your choice. (For comment on edges, see technical note on page 44)

Remember to center your stitch patterns or adjust the stitch count as necessary when you begin each new pattern (see pages 33 to 35).

Repeat from * 4 times, or until the end of the scarf measures approximately ____ inches (cm) (**end length**).

Work 3 garter ridges (6 rows).

❸ Work center ribbed section

You need an odd number of stitches. If you have an even number of stitches, decrease 1 stitch; you can do this by working one k2tog in place of a knit stitch in the middle of your first row of ribbing.

Work in k1, p1 ribbing as follows:

Row 1: K1, *p1, k1. Repeat from * to end of row.

Row 2: P1, *k1, p1. Repeat from * to end of row.

Repeat rows 1 and 2 until center portion of scarf measures 12 inches (30.5 cm).

If you decreased 1 stitch for the ribbing, increase 1 stitch so that you have the same number of stitches in the second end as you did in the first end. You can do this by increasing 1 stitch in the middle of your last row of ribbing—don't worry that the added stitch will interrupt the ribbing pattern; just maintain the established sequence, matching the previous row, for the rest of the row.

❹ Work second end

Work as for the first end, reversing the order of the pattern stitches for balance.

❺ Bind off

Bind off loosely. Weave in the ends.

Pullover with Single Motif

This is the most basic sweater in this book. Knitted in stockinette stitch with a single motif on the front, it is a perfect project for you to try if you've never designed your own sweater or knitted in the round. For the ultimate in simplicity, skip the motif and knit this sweater in plain stockinette stitch using a gorgeous multicolored or textured yarn.

← Single motif on upper body

✓ Texture stitches: optional single motif on stockinette background, with ribbing at lower edge

✓ Lower body worked in the round and upper body sections worked back and forth

✓ Shallow square neckline, finished with picked-up ribbing

✓ Sleeves picked up at armholes and knitted down to ribbed cuffs

The illustration above shows a sweater with a 40-inch (101.6-cm) body circumference and 24-inch (61-cm) body length (including 2 inches [5 cm] of ribbing) in chunky-weight yarn with 3½ stitches and 5 rows to the inch (14 stitches and 20 rows to 10 cm). The illustration opposite shows a sweater of the same size in worsted-weight yarn with 5 stitches and 7 rows to the inch (20 stitches and 28 rows to 10 cm).

Get ready   *yarn & needles*

Yarn

As with the seaman's scarf, a smooth yarn will show off the purl-stitch texture of the motif featured on the front of this sweater. If you are including the motif, don't use a thick-and-thin or fuzzy yarn, which will obscure the pattern.

Any weight of yarn will work, but for practice I suggest a medium-weight yarn and U.S. size 7 or 8 (4.5 or 5 mm) knitting needles.

Needle guidelines are on page 22. See the yarn estimate table on page 23 for yardages.

Knitting needles

In a size appropriate for the yarn you've chosen:

+ Circular needle for body: for most adult sweaters, you will want a needle at least 29 inches (74 cm) long

+ Circular needle for sleeves and neckband: 16 inches (40 cm) long

+ Double-pointed needles for lower sleeves: set of 4 or 5

Optional for ribbings: Two sizes smaller than primary needles:

+ Circular needle for body ribbing: for most adult sweaters, you will want a needle at least 29 inches (74 cm) long

+ Double-pointed needles for cuff ribbing: set of 4 or 5

If you decide to use smaller needles for the ribbings, I'll count on you to know when to switch between needle sizes. Everyone else: Work on same-size needles with me. You'll do fine.

Get set *stitches, gauge & size*

Stitches and gauge

① Select the motif for your sweater. Use the anchor motif shown on page 39 or choose another motif from a knitting-stitch library.

If you choose a fine or bulky yarn, make a swatch of the full motif to be sure it is not so small that it won't show up or so large that it will not fit on the upper front of the sweater.

② Make a gauge swatch in stockinette stitch.

③ Measure your gauge. Write the stitch gauge and row gauge on the sweater-planning worksheet on page 53.

Size

① Measure your favorite sweater or use the size charts on page 16 to determine the basic dimensions for your sweater. Write the measurements on the visual plan on page 52 and the sweater-planning worksheet on page 53.

② Use the calculations on the worksheets on pages 53 and 54 to figure all the remaining numbers before you start, or just calculate each new number as you need it.

③ Transfer the resulting numbers to the visual plan on page 52 or the step-by-step instructions on pages 55 to 57, depending on how much guiding detail you would like to have while you knit.

Knit! *option I: using a visual plan*

For knitters who are ready to work from the basic concept

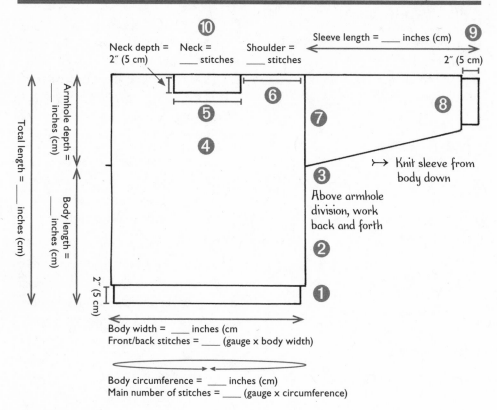

Neck depth = 2″ (5 cm)

Neck = ___ stitches

Shoulder = ___ stitches

Sleeve length = ___ inches (cm)

2″ (5 cm)

Armhole depth = ___ inches (cm)

Total length = ___ inches (cm)

Body length = ___ inches (cm)

2″ (5 cm)

Knit sleeve from body down

Above armhole division, work back and forth

Body width = ___ inches (cm
Front/back stitches = ___ (gauge x body width)

Body circumference = ___ inches (cm)
Main number of stitches = ___ (gauge x circumference)

BODY

1 Cast on ___ stitches (90% of main number of stitches) and knit ribbing

2 Increase to ___ stitches (main number of stitches), change to stockinette stitch, and work lower body

3 Separate for upper back and upper front

4 Work motif

5 Bind off center ___ neck stitches

6 Join shoulders: ___ stitches

SLEEVES

7 Pick up ___ sleeve stitches at armhole

8 Decrease to ___ cuff stitches

9 Work cuff ribbing and bind off

FINISH

10 Work neckband

Knit!	*option 2: using planning worksheets*	The Netherlands Pullover/Single Motif

For knitters who want to plan thoroughly in advance

Measurements

	Calculation	Example	Description
Stitch gauge	_____ stitches = 1 inch or 1 cm	**5** stitches = 1 inch	**Stitch gauge** is critical for knitting a sweater that fits properly.
Row gauge	_____ rows = 1 inch or 1 cm	**7** rows = 1 inch	**Row gauge** is not critical for this sweater.
Body width	_____ inches (cm)	**20** inches	Measure the **width** of the sweater body.
Body circumference	_____ x 2 = _____	20 x 2 = **40** inches	Double the body width for the **circumference of the sweater**.
Total length	_____ inches (cm)	**24** inches	Measure the **length** of the sweater body.
Sleeve length	_____ inches (cm)	**18** inches	Measure the **sleeve length** from wrist to underarm.
Armhole depth	_____ ÷ 4 = _____	40 ÷ 4 = **10** inches	Divide the body circumference by 4 to calculate the **armhole depth**.
Body length	_____ – _____ = _____	24 – 10 = **14** inches	Subtract the armhole depth from the total body length to calculate the **length of the body from the cast-on edge to the armhole**.
Sleeve circumference	_____ x 2 = _____	10 x 2 = **20** inches	Double the armhole depth for the **circumference of the sleeve**.

This example has been set up with numbers that clearly demonstrate the simple calculations. Those numbers happen to result in an adult's sweater with a finished chest measurement of 40″ (102 cm) that falls to a generous hip length. If you're not that size, and only a few of us will be, use the guidelines on pages 14 through 16 and measurements you gather for yourself to make a sweater that is customized for its wearer.

Stitch counts

		Calculation	Example	Description
a	Main number of stitches	___ x ___ = ___	40 x 5 = **200**	Multiply the body circumference by your stitch gauge to calculate the **main number of stitches**.
b	90% of main number of stitches	___ x 0.9 = ___	200 x 0.9 = **180**	Take 90 percent of the main number of stitches to calculate the **number of stitches to cast on**. If this is an odd number, add 1 so you have an even number of stitches for working the k1, p1 ribbing.
c	Front stitches & Back stitches	___ ÷ 2 = ___	200 ÷ 2 = **100**	Divide the main number of stitches in half to determine the **number of stitches in the upper front and upper back**.
d	Neck stitches & Shoulder stitches	___ ÷ 3 = ___	100 ÷ 3 = **33** 33 stitches for each shoulder, 34 stitches for neck	Divide the number of stitches in the upper front in thirds to calculate the **number of stitches in the neck and shoulders**. If your number of stitches is not a multiple of 3, include the extra stitch(es) with the neck. Make sure you have the same number of stitches in each shoulder.
	Motif stitches	___	**19**	The number of **stitches in the motif** you have chosen.
e	Motif side stitches	___ – ___ = ___ ___ ÷ 2 = ___	100 – 19 = **81** 80 ÷ 2 = **40**	Subtract the number of stitches in your motif from the number of stitches for the front. *Note:* If this is not an even number, decrease 1 stitch before beginning motif. Divide the result in half to calculate how to **center the motif**.
f	Sleeve stitches	___ x ___ = ___	20 x 5 = **100**	Multiply the sleeve circumference by your stitch gauge to calculate the **number of sleeve stitches** to pick up at the armhole.
g	Cuff stitches	___	**40**	After you knit the body of your sweater, wrap the ribbing around your wrist and count the **number of stitches for the cuff**. For a rough estimate of this number, divide the main number of stitches by 5.

Need a slightly different stitch count? Increase or decrease by a few.

Knit!	*option 3: a step-by-step project sheet*	The Netherlands Pullover/Single Motif

For knitters who would like detailed instructions

Use this project sheet if you are not yet comfortable working directly from the sweater-planning diagram. With time, you'll find that you no longer need to refer to these instructions.

Do the calculations on the planning worksheets on pages 53 and 54 so you have the numbers to fill in here.

❶ Cast on and knit ribbing

With a 29-inch (74 cm) circular needle, cast on ____ stitches (**90% of main number of stitches**). Join, being careful not to twist, and knit in the round.

Work in k1, p1 ribbing until the body measures 2 inches (5 cm), or until the ribbing is the desired length.

❷ Work lower body

Change to stockinette stitch (knit every round). Increase to ____ stitches (**main number of stitches**) on the first round as follows: *K9, increase 1, repeat from * to end of round.

On the next round, knit ____ **back stitches**, place a second marker, knit to the end of the round. You now have a marker at the beginning of the round and a second marker halfway around, marking the side "seams" of the sweater.

Work even in stockinette stitch until the body measures ____ inches (cm) (**body length**) from the cast-on edge.

❸ Separate for upper back and upper front

You will work the upper back and upper front back and forth on your circular needle, with half the stitches on hold as you work each section. (Place the stitches that are on hold on a piece of scrap yarn or a large stitch holder.)

Starting at the beginning of the round, knit across ____ **back stitches** to the first marker for the upper back. Place the remaining ____ **front stitches** on hold.

Upper back

On the back stitches, work back and forth in stockinette stitch (knit right-side rows; purl wrong-side rows) until the back of the sweater measures ____ inches (cm) (**total length**) from the cast-on edge.

Divide the back stitches into thirds. Work one more row on the back, and as you do so bind off the center ____ **neck stitches**.

You will have two sets of back shoulder stitches remaining active. Put these two sets of stitches on hold.

Upper front

Return the upper front stitches to active status on the needle. Join the yarn to the front so that the next row will be a right-side row. Work back and forth on the front stitches in stockinette stitch for 4 rows.

④ Work the motif

Knit _____ **motif side stitches,** place marker, work the motif chart, place marker, knit _____ **motif side stitches**.

Work the patterns as established, slipping markers when you come to them, until you have knitted all the rows of the motif chart.

Work even in stockinette stitch until the front is 2 inches (5 cm) shorter than the back.

⑤ Shape neckline on upper front

Divide the front stitches into thirds. As you work across the front stitches, bind off the center _____ **neck stitches**. Then work each of the two front shoulders separately in stockinette stitch until the front is as long as the back.

⑥ Join shoulders

Join the front and back at each shoulder using the three-needle bind-off.

⑦ Pick up stitches for sleeves

Beginning at the underarm and using the 16-inch (40-cm) circular needle, pick up _____ **sleeve stitches** around the armhole opening on one side of the sweater. Place a marker, join, and begin knitting stockinette stitch in the round.

⑧ Work sleeve decreases

AT THE SAME TIME, begin decreasing for the sleeve as follows: On every 4th round, k1, k2tog, knit to 3 stitches before the marker, ssk, k1.

When the stitches no longer fit comfortably on the circular needle, change to double-pointed needles.

Keep an eye on the shape of your sleeve and measure it against your model sweater or try your sweater on after every few inches (cm) to make sure the sleeve is decreasing at a comfortable rate. If your sleeve is becoming narrow too quickly, start decreasing every 6th round. If it is not narrowing quickly enough, start decreasing every 3rd round.

Continue decreasing until you have _____ **cuff stitches** and then work even.

When your sleeve measures 2 inches (5 cm) less than **sleeve length** (_____ inches [cm]), or _____ inches (cm), try on the sweater to test the sleeve length. The bottom of the sleeve should fall just above your wrist bone, to leave enough space to knit the cuffs.

If you have not decreased to _____ **cuff stitches** and your sleeve is the desired length to the start of the cuff, make the remaining number of decreases on the next round, spreading them evenly as you work the round.

⑨ Work cuff ribbing and bind off

Change to k1, p1 ribbing. Work in ribbing for 2 inches (5 cm).

Bind off loosely in pattern.

Make second sleeve the same way as the first, steps 7 through 9.

⑩ Finishing

Neckband

Starting at the left shoulder with the right side facing and using the 16-inch (40-cm) circular needle, pick up stitches down the left side of the neck front, across the bound-off stitches at the front neck, up the right side of the neck front, and across the bound-off stitches at the back neck.

If you have picked up an odd number of stitches, increase 1 stitch on the first round of the neckband so you have an even number of stitches for working the ribbing.

Work in k1, p1 ribbing for 1 inch (2.5 cm), or desired height of neckband. Bind off loosely in pattern.

Weave in the ends.

Tip for neckline edge: I bind off stitches at the neckline to give a firmer edge. Some knitters prefer to leave these stitches "live" and to incorporate them directly into the neck finish. On the next sweater, Project 3, which is finished with eyelets and a drawstring at the neckline, the stitches are left "live" so you can learn that technique as well.

Tip for picking up stitches: The basic guideline for picking up stitches comes from your gauge. For each inch (cm) of edge, pick up approximately the number of stitches in an inch (cm) of your gauge swatch, fudging, if necessary, on the "slightly less than" side.

Sampler Pullover

On this sampler fisherman's sweater, horizontal sweater patterns cover the body of the sweater and part of the sleeves. If you would like to simplify the design, work a large section of stockinette stitch above the ribbing and below the armholes and use only horizontal stripes on the yoke, or work the entire body and the sleeves in an easy check pattern (see page 40).

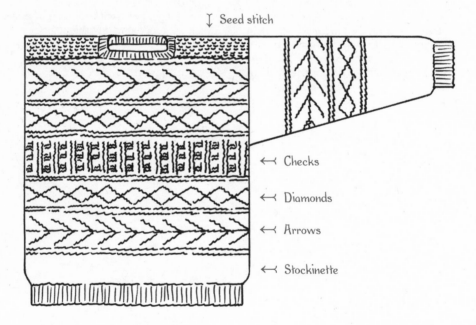

↧ Seed stitch

←⊣ Checks

←⊣ Diamonds

←⊣ Arrows

←⊣ Stockinette

✔ Texture stitches: horizontal bands

✔ Lower body worked in the round and
   upper body sections worked back and forth

✔ Shallow square neckline, finished with picked-up ribbing,
   plus optional eyelets and drawstring

✔ Sleeves picked up at armholes and knitted down to ribbed cuffs

The illustrations above and opposite show a sweater with a 40-inch (101.6-cm) body circumference and 24-inch (61-cm) body length (including 2 inches [5 cm] of ribbing) in heavy worsted-weight yarn with 4 stitches and 6 rows to the inch (16 stitches and 24 rows to 10 cm).

Get ready *yarn & needles*

Yarn

Select a smooth, tightly twisted yarn to make sure the pattern stitches pop out and show well. The design will be most visible if you choose a light color, but Dutch fishermen's sweaters were traditionally made in a variety of colors, so don't be afraid to experiment. If you are not sure the stitch pattern will show up adequately in the color you are considering, buy one ball of that yarn and make a swatch.

Any weight of yarn will work, but for practice I suggest a medium-weight yarn and U.S. size 7 or 8 (4.5 or 5 mm) needles. For a traditional sweater, select a lightweight yarn.

Needle guidelines are on page 22. See the yarn estimate table on page 23 for yardages.

Knitting needles

In a size appropriate for the yarn you've chosen:

✧ Circular needle for body: for most adult sweaters, you will want a needle at least 29 inches (74 cm) long

✧ Circular needle for sleeves and neckband: 16 inches (40 cm) long

✧ Double-pointed needles for lower sleeves: set of 4 or 5

Optional for ribbings: Two sizes smaller than primary needles:

✧ Circular needle for body ribbing: for most adult sweaters, you will want a needle at least 29 inches (74 cm) long

✧ Double-pointed needles for cuff ribbing: set of 4 or 5

If you decide to use smaller needles for the ribbings, I'll count on you to know when to switch between needle sizes. Everyone else: Work on same-size needles with me. You'll do fine.

Get set *stitches, gauge & size*

The Netherlands
Sampler Pullover

Stitches and gauge

① Select the stitches for your sweater. Use the combination shown on the sample sweater illustration, or choose your own combination of knit-and-purl pattern stitches. You may use all different pattern stitches, or repeat one or several pattern stitches.

② Make a gauge swatch in each of the pattern stitches you have chosen.

③ Measure your gauge. Each knit-and-purl pattern stitch will work up to a slightly different gauge, but the measurements will all be close so you can check the gauge of any swatch, or measure all of your swatches and take the average. Write the information on the sweater-planning worksheet on page 63.

④ Measure the height of each pattern-stitch swatch. Although row gauge is not critical in this sweater, knowing the total height of each of your chosen pattern stitches lets you know that your selections will fit within the length of the sweater body.

If you prefer, you can wing it, choosing your pattern stitches as you go. If you do this, the seed-stitch section at the shoulders may not be exactly 2 inches (5 cm) tall. If you are going to wing it, I trust that you can make the necessary adjustments, and I've added notes to help you throughout the pattern.

Size

① Measure your favorite sweater or use the size charts on page 16 to determine the basic dimensions for your sweater. Write the measurements on the visual plan on page 62 and the sweater-planning worksheet on page 63.

② Use the calculations on the worksheets on pages 63 and 64 to figure all the remaining numbers before you start, or just calculate each new number as you need it.

③ Transfer the resulting numbers to the visual plan on page 62 or the step-by-step instructions on pages 65 to 67, depending on how much guiding detail you would like to have while you knit.

The texture patterns inspired by sweaters from the Netherlands are on pages 38 to 41.

Knit! *option I: using a visual plan*

The Netherlands
Sampler Pullover

For knitters who are ready to work from the basic concept

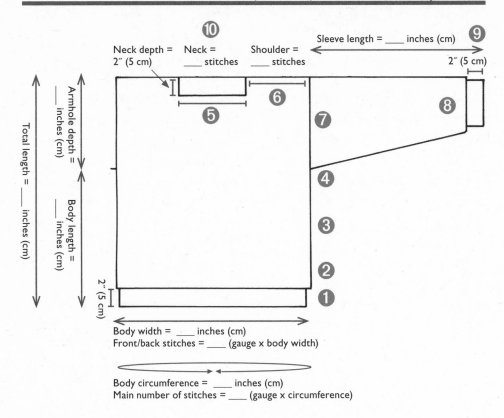

Neck depth = 2″ (5 cm)

Neck = ____ stitches

Shoulder = ____ stitches

Sleeve length = ____ inches (cm)

2″ (5 cm)

Armhole depth = ____ inches (cm)

Total length = ____ inches (cm)

Body length = ____ inches (cm)

2″ (5 cm)

Body width = ____ inches (cm)
Front/back stitches = ____ (gauge x body width)

Body circumference = ____ inches (cm)
Main number of stitches = ____ (gauge x circumference)

BODY

1. Cast on ____ stitches (90% of main number of stitches) and knit ribbing

2. Increase to ____ stitches (main number of stitches) and work lower body

3. Work pattern stitches

4. Separate for upper back and upper front

5. Bind off center ____ neck stitches

6. Join shoulders: ____ stitches

SLEEVES

7. Pick up ____ sleeve stitches at armhole

8. Decrease to ____ cuff stitches

9. Work cuff ribbing and bind off

FINISH

10. Work neckband

Knit! *option 2: using planning worksheets* The Netherlands Sampler Pullover

For knitters who want to plan thoroughly in advance

Measurements

	Calculation	Example	Description
Stitch gauge	____ stitches = 1 inch or 1 cm	**5** stitches = 1 inch	**Stitch gauge** is critical for knitting a sweater that fits properly.
Row gauge	____ rows = 1 inch or 1 cm	**7** rows = 1 inch	**Row gauge** is not critical for this sweater.
Body width	____ inches (cm)	**20** inches	Measure the **width** of the sweater body.
Body circumference	____ x 2 = ____	**20** x 2 = **40** inches	Double the body width for the **circumference of the sweater**.
Total length	____ inches (cm)	**24** inches	Measure the **length** of the sweater body.
Sleeve length	____ inches (cm)	**18** inches	Measure the **sleeve length** from wrist to underarm.
Armhole depth	____ ÷ 4 = ____	**40** ÷ 4 = **10** inches	Divide the body circumference by 4 to calculate the **armhole depth**.
Body length	____ – ____ = ____	**24** – **10** = **14** inches	Subtract the armhole depth from the total body length to calculate the **length of the body from the cast-on edge to the armhole**.
Sleeve circumference	____ x 2 = ____	**10** x 2 = **20** inches	Double the armhole depth for the **circumference of the sleeve**.
Height of patterns	____ + ____ + ____ + ____ = ____	**13** inches	The **height of all of your pattern stitches** added together.
Height of stockinette stitch	____ – ____ = ____	**24** – **13** = **11**	Subtract the total height of all of your pattern stitches from the total length.
	____ – 5 = ____	**11** – **5** = **6** inches	Subtract 5 inches (10 cm) to account for the ribbing at the bottom of the sweater, the seed-stitch section at the shoulders, and the garter ridges that separate the pattern stitches. The result is the **length of stockinette stitch** to knit directly above the ribbing.

You can fudge this and just make it up as you go if you prefer. |

Stitch counts

		Calculation	Example	Description
a	Main number of stitches	___ x ___ = ___	40 x 5 = **200**	Multiply the body circumference by your stitch gauge to calculate the **main number of stitches**.
b	90% of main number of stitches	___ x 0.9 = ___	200 x 0.9 = **180**	Take 90 percent of the main number of stitches to calculate the **number of stitches to cast on**. If this is an odd number, add 1 so you have an even number of stitches for working the k1, p1 ribbing.
c	Front stitches & Back stitches	___ ÷ 2 = ___	200 ÷ 2 = **100**	Divide the main number of stitches in half to determine the **number of stitches in the upper front and upper back**.
d	Neck stitches & Shoulder stitches	___ ÷ 3 = ___	100 ÷ 3 = **33** 33 sts for each shoulder, 34 sts for neck	Divide the number of stitches in the upper front in thirds to calculate the **number of stitches in the neck and shoulders**. If your number of stitches is not a multiple of 3, include the extra stitches with the neck. Make sure you have the same number of stitches in each shoulder.
e	Sleeve stitches	___ x ___ = ___	20 x 5 = **100**	Multiply the sleeve circumference by your stitch gauge to calculate the **number of sleeve stitches** to pick up at the armhole.
f	Cuff stitches	___	**40**	After you knit the body of your sweater, wrap the ribbing around your wrist and count the **number of stitches for the cuff**. For a rough estimate of this number, divide the main number of stitches by 5.

Need a slightly different stitch count? Increase or decrease by a few.

This example has been set up with numbers that clearly demonstrate the simple calculations. Those numbers happen to result in an adult's sweater with a finished chest measurement of 40″ (102 cm) that falls to a generous hip length. If you're not that size, and only a few of us will be, use the guidelines on pages 14 through 16 and measurements you gather for yourself to make a sweater that is customized for its wearer.

Knit! *option 3: a step-by-step project sheet*   The Netherlands
Sampler Pullover

For knitters who would like detailed instructions

Use this project sheet if you are not yet comfortable working directly from the sweater-planning diagram. With time, you'll find that you no longer need to refer to these instructions.

Do the calculations on the planning worksheets on pages 63 and 64 so you have the numbers to fill in here.

❶ Cast on and knit ribbing

 With a 29-inch (74-cm) circular needle, cast on ____ stitches (**90% of main number of stitches**). Join, being careful not to twist, and knit in the round.

Work in k1, p1 ribbing until the body measures 2 inches (5 cm), or until the ribbing is the desired length.

❷ Work lower body

 Change to stockinette stitch (knit every round). Increase to ____ stitches (**main number of stitches**) on the first round as follows: *K9, increase 1, repeat from * to end of round.

 On the next round, knit ____ **back stitches**, place a second marker, knit to the end of the round. You now have a marker at the beginning of the round and a second marker halfway around, marking the side "seams" of the sweater.

 Work even in stockinette stitch until the body measures ____ inches (cm) (**height**

of stockinette stitches**) from the cast-on edge. (Or work for the desired length, if you are winging it and choosing pattern stitches as you go.)

❸ Work patterns

*Work 2 garter ridges (4 rounds of garter stitch). Then work a full repeat of a horizontal stitch pattern of your choice.

When you begin each new pattern, remember to center your stitch patterns or adjust the stitch count as necessary (see pages 33 to 35).

Repeat from * until the body measures ____ inches (cm) (**body length**) from the cast-on edge.

❹ Separate for upper back and front

You will work the upper back and upper front back and forth on the larger circular needle, with half the stitches on hold as you work each section. (Place the stitches that are on hold on a piece of scrap yarn or a large stitch holder.)

Starting at the beginning of the round, work in pattern across ____ **back stitches** for the upper back. Place the remaining ____ **front stitches** on hold.

Upper back

On the back stitches, work back and forth, continuing to work the patterns, separating each pattern from the next with 2 garter ridges, until all planned patterns have been worked. The back should measure approximately 2 inches (5 cm) less than **total length** (____ inches [cm]), or ____ inches (cm). (Or if you are winging it, continue working pattern stitches until no more patterns will fit between the current position and the top of the back.)

Work 2 garter ridges.

Work in seed stitch for 2 inches (5 cm) or until the back of the sweater measures ____ inches (cm) (**body length**) from the cast-on edge.

Put the back stitches on hold.

Upper front

Return the upper front stitches to active status on the needle. Join the yarn to the front so that the next row will be a right-side row. Work back and forth on the front stitches, as you did for the back, until the front is 2 inches (5 cm) shorter than the back. (This should be just after you finish the garter ridge after the final pattern, unless you are winging it.)

⑤ **Shape neckline on upper front**

Divide the front stitches into thirds. Put the center ____ **neck stitches** on hold. Work the two shoulders separately until the front is as long as the back.

⑥ **Join shoulders**

Divide the back stitches into thirds. Put the center ____ **neck stitches** on hold. Join the front and back at the shoulders using the three-needle bind-off.

⑦ **Pick up stitches for sleeves**

Beginning at the underarm and using the 16-inch (40-cm) circular needle, pick up ____ **sleeve stitches** around the armhole opening on one side of the sweater. Place a marker, join, and begin knitting stockinette stitch in the round.

⑧ **Work sleeve patterns and sleeve decreases**

Work 3 inches (7.5 cm) in stockinette stitch. *Work 2 garter ridges. Work the pattern stitch of your choice. Repeat from * once more. Work 2 garter ridges. Work the remainder of the sleeve to the cuff in stockinette stitch.

AT THE SAME TIME, begin decreasing for the sleeve on the 4th round after picking up stitches as follows: On every 4th round, k1, k2tog, knit to 3 stitches before the marker, ssk, k1.

When the stitches no longer fit comfortably on the circular needle, change to double-pointed needles.

Keep an eye on the shape of your sleeve and measure it against your model sweater or try your sweater on after every few inches (cm) to make sure the sleeve is decreasing at a comfortable rate. If your sleeve is becoming narrow too quickly, start decreasing every 6th round. If it is not narrowing quickly enough, start decreasing every 3rd round.

Continue decreasing until you have ____ **cuff stitches** and then work even.

When your sleeve measures 2 inches (5 cm) less than **sleeve length** (____ inches

[cm]), or _____ inches (cm), try on the sweater to test the sleeve length. The bottom of the sleeve should fall just above your wrist bone, to leave enough space to knit the cuffs.

 If you have not decreased to _____ **cuff stitches** and your sleeve is the desired length to the start of the cuff, make the remaining number of decreases on the next round, spreading them evenly as you work the round.

⑨ Work cuff ribbing and bind off

Change to k1, p1 ribbing. Work in ribbing for 2 inches (5 cm).

Bind off loosely in pattern.

Make second sleeve the same way as the first, steps 7 through 9.

⑩ Finishing

Neckband with optional eyelets for a drawstring

Starting at the left shoulder with the right side facing and using the 16-inch (40-cm) circular needle, pick up stitches down the left side of the neck front, knit across the front stitches on hold, pick up stitches up the right side of the neck front, and knit across the back stitches on hold.

If you end up with an odd number of stitches, increase 1 stitch on the first

~~~~~~~~~~~~~~~~~~~

Tip: The basic guideline for picking up stitches comes from your gauge. For each inch (cm) of edge, pick up approximately the number of stitches in an inch (cm) of your gauge swatch, fudging on the "slightly less than" side.

round of the neckband so you have an even number of stitches for working the ribbing.

Work in k1, p1 ribbing for ½ inch (1.25 cm), or half of the desired height of the neckband.

If desired, add eyelets for a drawstring as follows: On the next round *ssk, yo. Repeat from * to end of round.

Work in k1, p1 ribbing until the neckband is the desired height.

Bind off loosely in pattern.

Weave in the ends.

Optional drawstring

Make a twisted cord to use as a drawstring as follows:

1. Cut several pieces of yarn about 5 times the desired length of the finished drawstring and knot the strands together at both ends.

2. Attach one end to a hook or a doorknob and twist the strands until they begin to kink. Remove the end of the yarn from the hook, being careful not to let the yarn untwist or snarl.

3. Holding the yarn in the center, fold the twisted strand so the ends come together. Now allow the strands to twist back on themselves. They will naturally twist together in the direction opposite to the twist you added.

4. Tie the open end of the drawstring with a knot. Weave the drawstring through the eyelets in the neckband.

5 If you would like, make and add pompoms to ends of drawstring (page 80).

Denmark

Denmark was the first Scandinavian country to embrace knitting—doing so at least as early as the sixteenth century. A knitting-needle holder in the collection of the National Museum in Copenhagen dates from around 1570 to 1580. The oldest known piece of Danish knitting that remains is a fragment from the seventeenth century.

The craft, probably imported from Germany or the Netherlands, was quickly adopted and Danish knitters began to create striking garments and accessories decorated with intricate knit-and-purl texture patterns. Danish knitters' tastes proved to be amazingly constant. Patterns used in the seventeenth century remained popular into the twentieth century.

In the past, Danish women, children, and sometimes men knitted underwear, nightclothes, stockings, leggings, gloves, mittens, and caps. Originally, men and women collected wool when the local sheep shed naturally in the spring, or they sometimes plucked the wool directly from the sheep's backs. (This can only be done with primitive-style sheep, who do shed.) They combed the wool so that all of the fibers were parallel, and then spun a very smooth and fine yarn that enhanced the textured stitch patterns of their knitting. Items were often dyed solid colors after they were knitted. The most popular color for Danish knitted blouses was red, followed by blue and green.

Danish blouses with knit-and-purl patterning trace their origins to nightshirts and undershirts. Today it is amazing to think that people would put so much time and energy into creating ornate garments that would never be seen in public. But before mass-produced clothing was available, there was no choice but to make everything for yourself and your family. If you are going to knit a nightshirt, why not add a texture pattern to keep from getting bored with row after row of plain stockinette stitch?

While silk shirts were popular with the upper classes for a

These Danish sweaters build on the previous chapter's skills. They have more complex patterning and shaping.

short time in the seventeenth century, woolen nightshirts, called *nattrøjer*, were commonly worn by people of all classes for centuries. These nightshirts doubled as undershirts for those who could not afford two separate garments. The earliest *nattrøjer* were worn by both men and women. Over time, men stopped wearing them and the *nattrøjer* evolved into a short, body-hugging style that accentuated a woman's figure and complemented the traditional Danish woman's costume. The transition went to the extreme around 1800, when the empire-waist style was popular through most of Europe and these knitted garments were sometimes made as short as 12 inches (30.5 cm).

Some knitters in Denmark decorated their blouses with fabric trim, ribbons, or appliqués at the neck and cuffs. Other knitters used simple knit-and-purl patterns at the waist, neckline, and cuffs

Chapter

4

CHAPTER HIGHLIGHTS

Skills

- ✓ Knit-and-purl texture patterning worked both in the round and back and forth

Techniques

- ✓ Centering horizontal patterns

- ✓ Centering an all-over pattern

- ✓ Welts at lower body edges

- ✓ Half-gussets (optional)

Garment styling

- ✓ Drop shoulder, either standard pullover style or fitted at waist

- ✓ Upper body sections worked back and forth

- ✓ Sleeves knitted from cuff to shoulder and sewn onto body to frame a sweater. Small, easy patterns were frequently used on portions of the sweater that would be tucked in or covered by other garments, while knitters worked large, ornate designs on the main bodice and sleeves.

Because the climate was cold and a single layer of textured knitting did not provide the extra warmth of the two-color knitting that became popular in other parts of Scandinavia, some Danish knitters sewed wool fleece inside the sleeves of their sweaters. For extra warmth, women also wore heavy knitted petticoats that were often so thick the garments would stand up on their own!

The Danish blouse is knitted from the bottom up, in a combination of back-and-forth and in-the-round techniques. The sweater is begun flat, with front and back welts (or decorative strips) that are worked separately in garter stitch or a simple knit-and-purl pattern. After the welts are joined together, the main body of the sweater is knitted in the round to the armholes. The sweater fits closely at the waist, and increases worked at the sides widen the sweater to fit the bust. Half-gussets can be worked at the underarms to provide flexibility. At the armholes, the sweater is again divided into front and back sections and the upper body pieces are knitted back and forth. A square neckline is framed with a simple knit-and-purl pattern to coordinate with the welts, and no added neckband is needed.

When the body has been completed, the shoulders are joined by the three-needle bind-off. The sleeves are usually worked separately from cuff to shoulder and then sewn to the body, although there is no reason that a knitter cannot pick up stitches at the shoulders and knit the sleeves down to the cuffs to avoid the need for sewing.

The word welt *has several meanings in the world of knitting. In this case, it refers to strips of fabric that run horizontally at the bottoms of the front and back sections of the sweater. Sometimes welt means a horizontal ridge of fabric—like ribbing, except that welts run across the fabric as they are worked.*

A bit of knitting-style history

Until the nineteenth century, most Danish knitters used the English method of knitting, with the yarn carried in the right hand and thrown around the tip of the needle to create each stitch. Today, however, Continental knitting is ubiquitous in Denmark and most knitters carry the yarn in the left hand and it is picked up to form the stitches. Either method works to create knit-and-purl stitch patterns, but many knitters find it easier to move the yarn to the back for knits and to the front for purls using the lefthand carry.

Techniques

Overlapping welts

The welts at the bottom of a Danish blouse are worked separately. After both welts have been finished, the knitter joins them at the sides and then continues working the body in the round.

To join the welts:

1. Overlap the welts, placing last 2 stitches of the front welt on top of the first 2 stitches of the back welt. Purl 2 together twice, each time picking up 1 stitch from the front welt and 1 stitch from the back welt.

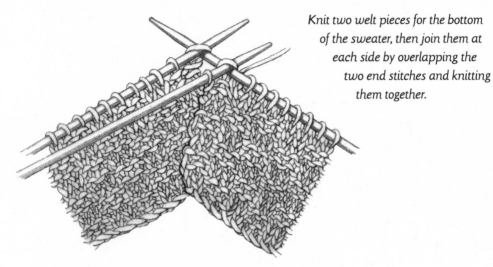

Knit two welt pieces for the bottom of the sweater, then join them at each side by overlapping the two end stitches and knitting them together.

2. Knit across the rest of the front welt until 2 stitches remain. You have worked one-half of a round.

3. Repeat steps 1 and 2. You should now be at the beginning of the round.

As you continue working the garment, on each round continue to purl the 2 stitches at each side that you used to join the welts. These columns of purl stitches create a visual side "seam."

Underarm half-gussets

Underarm gussets give snug sweaters more wiggle room. The type of gusset used in the sweaters in this chapter, called a half-gusset, consists of a small triangle that is added to the body just below the beginning of the armhole. The extra stitches in this triangle become part of the armhole opening.

Start a half-gusset approximately 1 inch (2.5 cm) below underarm level:

1. Work in pattern to the first 2-stitch purl column. Increase 1 stitch between the 2 purl stitches. Repeat at the second 2-stitch purl column on the other side of the garment.

2. Work the first gusset round as follows: Work in pattern to first purl-column stitch. Purl 1, increase 1, knit across to next purl-column stitch, increase 1, purl 1. Repeat at second purl-column set of stitches.

3. Repeat step 2 until body measures desired length from cast-on edge to underarm.

You work the gusset between the two purl stitches at the side. One purl stitch stays with each body section.

Sleeve will
be here

↓ Half-gusset

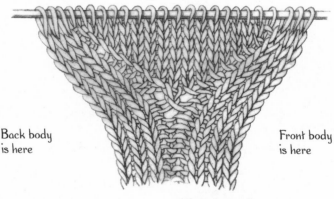

Back body
is here

Front body
is here

↑ Side "seam"

Pattern stitches

Small checks

Repeat: 4 stitches by 4 rows

Large checks

Repeat:
8 stitches by 8 rows

Diagonals

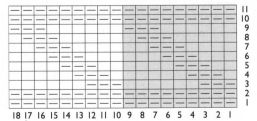

Repeat: 9 stitches by 11 rows

73

Seed-stitch triangles

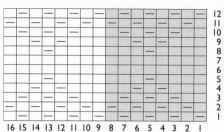

Repeat: 8 stitches by 12 rows

Solid triangles

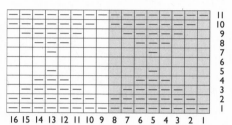

Repeat: 8 stitches by 11 rows

Eight-point rose all-over pattern

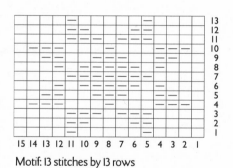

Motif: 13 stitches by 13 rows

The sources from which I obtained these designs call them "roses," although they are virtually identical to "star" and "snowflake" designs from other areas.

The small rose motif is 13 stitches wide. The chart is shown with a 15-stitch width as a reminder that the figure needs to be set off by stockinette stitch on all sides (including above and below the motif).

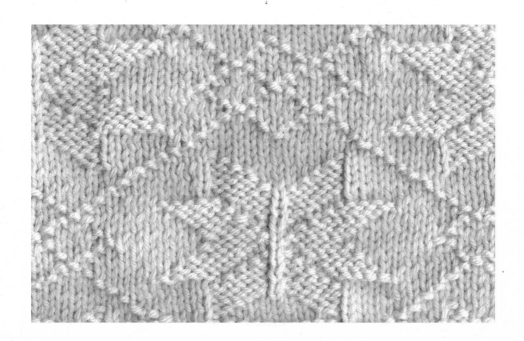

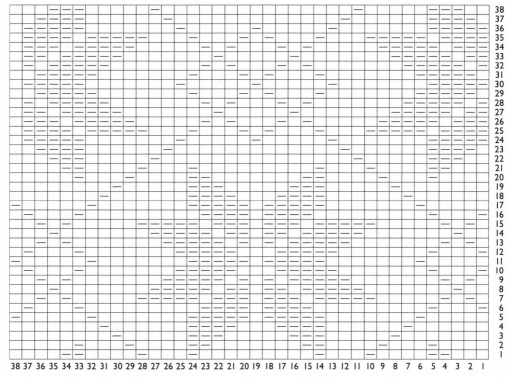

Repeat: 38 stitches by 38 rows

Cap

*From as early as 1550 until around 1860, Danish men
wore knitted nightcaps. Making a cap of this type, knitted in the round, will give you a chance to practice circular knitting and knit-and-purl stitch patterns. If you use
the same yarn you plan to use for a sweater, your cap
can also serve as a large gauge swatch.*

*This simple style is as popular today as it was in the six-
teenth century. The brim begins with a simple knit-and-
purl pattern. Then the body of the hat incorporates more
elaborate texture designs. When you reach the crown,
you change to plain stockinette stitch to make it easy
to work the decreases. If you are not yet proficient with
double-pointed needles, the crown will give you practice.
If you knit a cap before you do a sweater, you'll be
comfortable with double-points by the time you
need to work the cuffs of your sweater sleeves.*

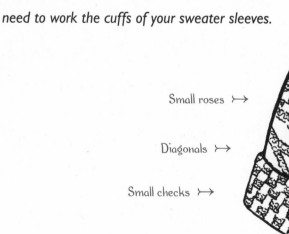

Small roses ⟼

Diagonals ⟼

Small checks ⟼

✓ Texture stitches worked in the round

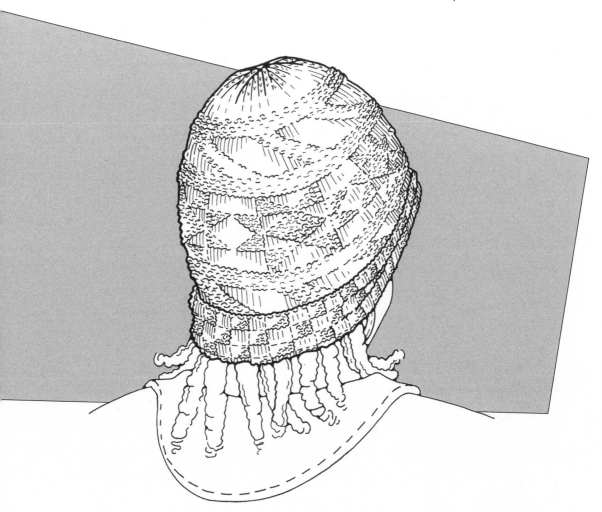

The illustration above shows a hat with a 20-inch (50.5-cm) body circumference and 10-inch (25.5-cm)

length to the crown (including 3 inches [7.5 cm] of brim) in chunky-weight yarn with 3½ stitches

and 5 rows to the inch (14 stitches and 20 rows to 10 cm). The illustration opposite shows a hat of the

same dimensions worked in worsted-weight yarn with 5 stitches and 7 rows to the inch (20 stitches

and 28 rows to 10 cm). At the smaller gauge, more repeats of the small rose pattern fit around the

head and there's an extra set of diagonals adjacent to the brim.

Get ready   *yarn & needles*

Yarn

Smooth yarn will show off texture patterns best. Choose a tightly spun yarn to make a warm, weatherproof cap, or a loosely spun yarn to make a softer cap.

Any weight of yarn will work, but for practice I suggest a medium-weight yarn and U.S. size 7 or 8 (4.5 or 5 mm) knitting needles. Approximately 200 yards (182 m) of medium-weight yarn will make a medium-sized adult cap.

Knitting needles

In a size appropriate for the yarn you've chosen:

✧ Circular needle: 16 inches (40 cm) long

✧ Double-pointed needles: set of 4 or 5

Needle guidelines are on page 22.

Get set   *stitches, gauge & size*

Stitches and gauge

① Select the stitches for your cap. Use the combination shown on the sample illustrations (pages 76 and 77), or choose your own combination of knit-and-purl pattern stitches from a stitch dictionary or through experimentation.

② Make a gauge swatch in each of the pattern stitches you have chosen.

③ Measure your stitch gauge. Each knit-and-purl pattern stitch will work up to a slightly different gauge, but the measurements will be close enough that for the basic shaping calculations you can take the gauge of any swatch, or measure all of your swatches and take the average. You will also want to eyeball the heights of

your patterns to determine whether they will fit within the length of your cap, and to help you decide the sequence in which you think they will look best to you.

Size

① Select a size for your cap and write the measurements in the boxes on the planning worksheet on page 80. These caps fit snugly. If you want a looser cap, add 1 or 2 inches (a few centimeters) to the circumference.

② Use the calculations on the worksheet to figure your cast-on number.

③ Transfer the numbers to the visual plan and the step-by-step instructions.

⁂ Child: 16-inch (40.6-cm) circumference

⁂ Adult medium: 18-inch (45.7-cm) circumference

⁂ Adult large: 20-inch (50.8-cm) circumference

Knit! *option I: using a visual plan*   Denmark Cap

For knitters who are ready to work from the basic concept

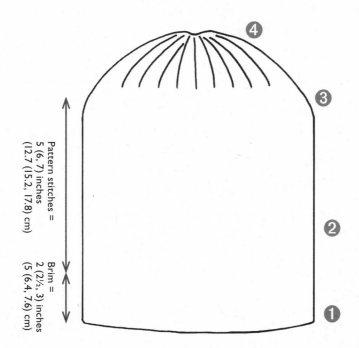

Pattern stitches =
5 (6, 7) inches
(12.7 (15.2, 17.8) cm)

Brim =
2 (2½, 3) inches
(5 (6.4, 7.6) cm)

① Cast on ＿＿ stitches and work brim

② Work pattern stitches

③ Work crown decreases, changing to double-pointed needles as needed

④ Finish

Knit! *option 2: using planning worksheets* Denmark Cap

For knitters who want to plan thoroughly in advance

Measurements and stitch counts

	Calculation	Example	Description
Stitch gauge	___ stitches = 1 inch or 1 cm	**5** stitches = 1 inch	Knitting is elastic, so there is some leeway, but **stitch gauge** is important for knitting a cap that fits correctly.
Circumference	___ inches (cm)	**20** inches	Desired **circumference** of cap.
Main number of stitches	___ x ___ = ___	20 x 5 = **100**	Multiply the circumference by your stitch gauge to calculate the **main number of stitches**.

Keep in mind that you will want your main number of stitches to be a multiple of your pattern stitches, and that you may need to adjust the stitch count slightly between patterns. See pages 34 to 35.

Optional pompom(s) (Projects 3 and 4)

Make pompoms as follows:

1. Cut a 2-inch-wide (5-cm) rectangle out of stiff cardboard.

2. Wrap yarn around the cardboard 40 or 50 times. The more wraps you make, the fuller your pompom will be. Cut the yarn.

3. At one edge of the cardboard, tie the strands of pompom together tightly with a 6-inch (15-cm) piece of yarn.

4. Along the opposite edge of the cardboard, cut the yarn strands of the pompom open and remove the cardboard.

5. Fluff the pompom and trim to neaten it up.

Attach one pompom to the top of the cap (project 3) or to each end of the drawstring (project 4).

Knit! *option 3: a step-by-step project sheet*

Denmark
Cap

For knitters who would like detailed instructions

Do the calculations on the planning worksheet on page 80 so you have the numbers to fill in here.

① Cast on and work brim

Cast on ____ stitches (**main number of stitches**). Join, being careful not to twist, and knit in the round.

Work in ribbing (k1, p1 or k2, p2), seed stitch (page 38), or small checks (page 73) until the brim measures 2 (2½, 3) inches (5 [6.4, 7.6] cm).

② Work pattern stitches

Work in the pattern stitches of your choice until the hat measures 5 (6, 7) inches (12.7 [15.2, 17.8] cm) from the top of the brim, or the desired length to the crown.

Remember to center your stitch patterns or adjust the stitch count as necessary when you begin each new pattern (see pages 33 to 35).

③ Work crown

Change to double-pointed needles when the stitches no longer fit comfortably on the circular needle.

Begin working in stockinette stitch (knit every round). On the first round, work enough decreases so you have a total number of stitches that is a multiple of 4.

Decrease round 1: (K2, k2tog) around.

Work even in stockinette stitch for about 1 inch (2.5 cm).

Decrease round 2: (K2tog, k1) around.

Work even in stockinette stitch for about 1 inch (2.5 cm).

Decrease round 3: K1, then k2tog around. If you have an extra stitch, knit it.

Knit 1 round even.

K2tog repeatedly until 12 stitches or fewer remain.

④ Finishing

Cut the yarn and draw its tail through the remaining stitches. Fasten off.

Weave in the ends.

If you like, you can make a pompom and sew it to the top of the hat. See bottom of opposite page for pompom instructions.

Pullover with Simple Patterns

*Knitted in a simple check pattern with garter-stitch
welts, neck trim, and cuffs, this sweater is simple enough
that you will be able to relax as you knit. If you've never
worked with all-over knit-and-purl stitch patterns, this
sweater is a good first project for trying out this design
technique.*

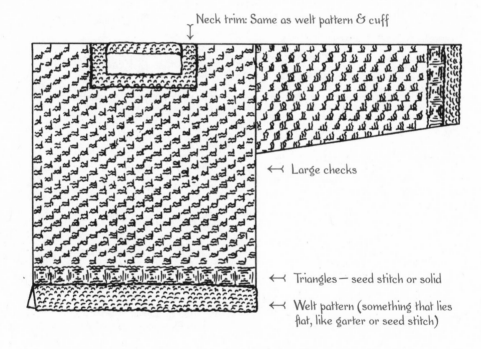

Neck trim: Same as welt pattern & cuff

←⊢ Large checks

←⊢ Triangles — seed stitch or solid

←⊢ Welt pattern (something that lies
flat, like garter or seed stitch)

✓ Simple texture patterns: all-over and horizontal bands

✓ Lower body worked in the round, with bottom welts,
   and upper body sections worked back and forth

✓ Relaxed body fit and wide sleeves

✓ Square neckline, with finishing trim knitted all-in-one with body

✓ Sleeves knitted from texture-stitch lower edge to shoulder and sewn on

This illustration shows a sweater with a 40-inch (101.6-cm) body circumference and 24-inch (61-cm) body length (including 2-inch [5-cm] welts) in worsted-weight yarn with 5 stitches and 7 rows to the inch (20 stitches and 28 rows to 10 cm). Experiment with chunky or fine yarns—use a bit of extra ease with heavy yarns. See tip on page 89 about welt and cuff edging patterns.

Get ready *yarn & needles*

Yarn

As for the cap on page 76, a smooth yarn will show off the texture stitches featured on this sweater. The check pattern will pop when knitted with a tightly spun solid yarn, but it will also be beautiful when worked in a multicolored or lightly textured yarn.

A thick-and-thin or fuzzy yarn is not suitable because you won't be able to see the texture of the stitches very well.

Any weight of yarn will work, but for practice I suggest a medium-weight yarn and U.S. size 7 or 8 (4.5 or 5 mm) knitting needles.

Needle guidelines are on page 22. See the yarn estimate table on page 23 for yardages.

Knitting needles

In a size appropriate for the yarn you've chosen:

✧ Circular needle for body: for most adult sweaters, you will want a needle at least 29 inches (74 cm) long

✧ Circular needle for sleeves and neckband: 16 inches (40 cm) long

✧ Double-pointed needles for lower sleeves: set of 4 or 5

Two sizes smaller than primary needles:

✧ Straight needles or circular needle for welts; if you use a circular needle, it should be at least 16 inches (40 cm) long

✧ Double-pointed needles for cuffs: set of 4 or 5

Get set   *stitches, gauge & size*

Stitches and gauge

① Select pattern stitches for your sweater. Use the stitches shown in the sample sweater illustration, or choose alternative motifs from a stitch dictionary or through experimentation.

② Make a gauge swatch in your main pattern stitch.

③ Measure your gauge. Write the stitch gauge and row gauge on the sweater-planning worksheet on page 87.

> The texture patterns inspired by sweaters from Denmark are on pages 73 to 75.

Size

① Measure your favorite sweater or use the size charts on page 16 to determine the basic dimensions for your sweater. Write the measurements on the visual plan on page 86 and the sweater-planning worksheet on page 87.

② Use the calculations on the worksheets on pages 87 and 88 to figure all the remaining numbers before you start, or just calculate each new number as you need it.

③ Transfer the resulting numbers to the visual plan on page 86 or the step-by-step instructions on pages 89 to 91, depending on how much guiding detail you would like to have while you knit.

Knit! *option I: using a visual plan*

Denmark
Simple Pullover

For knitters who are ready to work from the basic concept

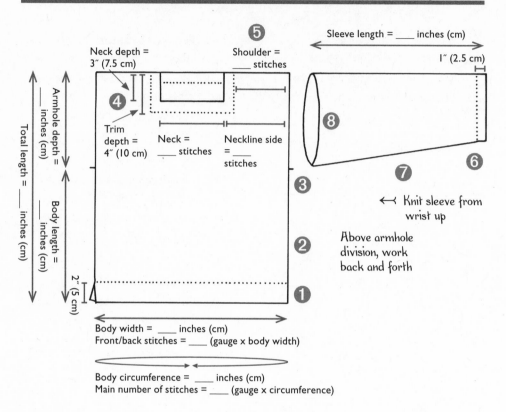

Neck depth =
3″ (7.5 cm)

Shoulder =
____ stitches

Sleeve length = ____ inches (cm)

1″ (2.5 cm)

Armhole depth =
—— inches (cm)

Total length = —— inches (cm)

Body length =
—— inches (cm)

Trim depth =
4″ (10 cm)

Neck =
____ stitches

Neckline side = ____ stitches

2″ (5 cm)

Knit sleeve from wrist up

Above armhole division, work back and forth

Body width = ____ inches (cm)
Front/back stitches = ____ (gauge x body width)

Body circumference = ____ inches (cm)
Main number of stitches = ____ (gauge x circumference)

BODY

❶ Cast on ____ stitches (welt stitches) and knit welts; join

❷ Work lower body

❸ Separate for upper back and upper front

❹ Work neck trim (____ neck trim stitches each side) and opening: ____ stitches

❺ Join shoulders: ____ stitches

SLEEVES

❻ Cast on ____ stitches and knit cuffs

❼ Increase to ____ sleeve stitches

❽ Sew in sleeves

Knit!	*option 2: using planning worksheets*		Denmark
			Simple Pullover

For knitters who want to plan thoroughly in advance

Measurements

	Calculation	Example	Description
Stitch gauge	____ stitches = 1 inch or 1 cm	**5** stitches = 1 inch	**Stitch gauge** is critical for knitting a sweater that fits properly.
Row gauge	____ rows = 1 inch or 1 cm	**7** rows = 1 inch	**Row gauge** is not critical for this sweater.
Body width	____ inches (cm)	**20** inches	Measure the **width** of the sweater body.
Body circumference	____ x 2 = ____ inches	20 x 2 = **40** inches	Double the body width for the **circumference of the sweater**.
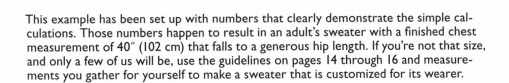 *Total length*	____ inches (cm)	**24** inches	Measure the **length** of the sweater body.
Sleeve length	____ inches (cm)	**18** inches	Measure the **sleeve length** from wrist to underarm.
Armhole depth	____ ÷ 4 = ____ inches	40 ÷ 4 = **10** inches	Divide the body circumference by 4 to calculate the **armhole depth**.
Body length	____ – ____ = ____ inches	24 – 10 = **14** inches	Subtract the armhole depth from the total body length to calculate the **length of the body from the cast-on edge to the armhole**.
Sleeve circumference	____ x 2 = ____ inches	10 x 2 = **20** inches	Double the armhole depth for the **circumference of the sleeve**.

A

B

C

This example has been set up with numbers that clearly demonstrate the simple calculations. Those numbers happen to result in an adult's sweater with a finished chest measurement of 40″ (102 cm) that falls to a generous hip length. If you're not that size, and only a few of us will be, use the guidelines on pages 14 through 16 and measurements you gather for yourself to make a sweater that is customized for its wearer.

Stitch counts

		Calculation	Example	Description
a	Main number of stitches	___ x ___ = ___	40 x 5 = **200**	Multiply the body circumference by your stitch gauge to calculate the **main number of stitches**.
b	Welt stitches Upper front & Upper back stitches	___ ÷ 2 = ___	200 ÷ 2 = **100**	Divide the main number of stitches in half to calculate both the **number of stitches to cast on for each welt** and the **number of stitches in the upper front and upper back**. For the welt, round off to the nearest multiple of the welt pattern stitch, if necessary. See *tip on the next page.*
c	Neck stitches & Shoulder stitches	___ ÷ 3 = ___	100 ÷ 3 = **33** with 1 extra **33** stitches for each shoulder; **34** stitches for neck	Divide the number of stitches in the upper front in thirds to calculate the **number of stitches in the neck and shoulders**. If your number of stitches is not a multiple of 3, include the extra stitches with the neck. Make sure you have the same number of stitches in each shoulder.
d	Neck trim stitches	___ + ___ = ___	34 + 10 = **44**	Add 2 inches' (5 cm) worth of stitches to the number of stitches in the neck. This is the **number of stitches in your neck trim**.
e	Neckline side stitches	___ − ___ = ___ ___ ÷ 2 = ___	100 − 44 = 56 56 ÷ 2 = **28**	Subtract the number of stitches in your neck trim from the number of stitches for the front. If this is an odd number, decrease 1 stitch. Divide the result in half to calculate the **neck side stitches** (to center the neckline).
f	Sleeve stitches	___ x ___ = ___	20 x 5 = **100**	Multiply the sleeve circumference by your stitch gauge to calculate the **number of sleeve stitches** needed at the top of the sleeve.
g	Cuff stitches	___	**60**	After you knit the body of your sweater, wrap the ribbing very loosely around your wrist and count the **number of stitches for the cuff**. This sweater is meant to have a very loose-fitting cuff.

Need a slightly different stitch count? Increase or decrease by a few.

Knit! *option 3: a step-by-step project sheet*

Denmark
Simple Pullover

For knitters who would like detailed instructions

Use this project sheet if you are not yet comfortable working directly from the sweater-planning diagram. With time, you'll find that you no longer need to refer to these instructions.

Do the calculations on the planning worksheets on pages 87 and 88 so you have the numbers to fill in here.

❶ Cast on and knit welts

With the smaller circular needle(s), cast on ____ stitches (**welt stitches; see tip below**).

Work in garter stitch or the pattern stitch of your choice until the welt measures 2 inches (5 cm).

Make a second welt to match the first.

Join welts to begin working in the round (see technique on page 71).

❷ Work lower body

Change to the larger circular needle. When you reach the 2 purl "seam" stitches at the first join of the welt sections, purl these 2 overlapped stitches. Knit across the first welt section. Purl the 2 overlapped stitches at the second join of the welt sections, on the other side of the sweater. Knit across the second welt section. You now have 2 purl stitches marking each side "seam" of the sweater. Continue to purl these 2 stitches that mark each side on every round.

On the first round after joining the welts, increase to ____ stitches (**main number of stitches**). (Remember that you "lost" 4 stitches in the overlapping join between the welts.)

Work all rows of a triangle pattern (page 74) and then switch to the large (4x4) check pattern (page 73)—or use the pattern stitches of your choice.

Remember to center your stitch patterns (see pages 33 to 34).

Work even in pattern, still continuing to purl the 2 stitches at each side, until the body measures ____ inches (cm) (**body length**) from the cast-on edge.

Tip: Welts are often worked in a pattern stitch that spreads out a bit, like garter stitch or seed stitch. You can simply let your welts and cuffs flare, if you like, or you can compensate. One way to compensate is to work the welts on smaller-sized needles, as described here. Another is to cast on slightly fewer stitches. Start with smaller needles and the number of stitches specified. Adjust if necessary to accommodate your choice of welt patterns. Remember that when you join the two welt sections you will "lose" 4 stitches

③ Separate for upper back and upper front

You will work the upper back and upper front back and forth on the larger circular needle, with half the stitches on hold as you work each section. (Place the stitches that are on hold on a piece of scrap yarn or a large stitch holder.)

Separate the knitting into front and back, placing the separation points at each side between the 2 purl stitches. In each section, there will be ____ **upper front** and **upper back stitches**. Each section should have 1 purl stitch on each end. Put one section on hold for the front, and leave the remaining stitches on the needle to work the upper back.

Upper back, including neckline trim

Work back and forth in pattern until the back of the sweater measures 1 inch (2.5 cm) less than **total length** (____ inches [cm]), or ____ inches (cm).

Work ____ **neckline side stitches**, place marker, work ____ **neck trim stitches** in the same pattern stitch used on the welts, place marker, work ____ **neckline side stitches**.

Continue to work patterns as established, slipping markers when you come to them, until the back measures ____ inches (cm) (**total length**). Bind off the center back ____ **neck stitches**. You will have 1 inch (2.5 cm) worth of neck trim stitches remaining active on each side of the bound-off stitches. Make sure you have the same number of stitches on each shoulder and in the neck trim on each side of the neck. Place each set of shoulder plus active neck-trim stitches on hold.

Upper front, including neckline trim

Put the upper-front stitches back on the needle. Join the yarn to the front so the next row will be a right-side row. Work back and forth in pattern until the front measures 4 inches (10 cm) less than **total length** (____ inches [cm]), or ____ inches (cm).

Begin the neckline trim as for the back and work until the trim measures 1 inch (2.5 cm). The front should now be 3 inches (7.5 cm) shorter than the back. Bind off the center front ____ **neck stitches**, making sure you have the same number of stitches on each shoulder and in the neck trim on each side of the neck and that these numbers match the number of stitches on hold for the back.

④ Shape neckline on upper front

Work each of the 2 shoulders separately in pattern as established until the front is as long as the back.

⑤ Join shoulders

Join the front and back at each shoulder using the three-needle bind-off. Join both shoulder and front neck-trim stitches on each side. The neck-trim stitches on the front should line up with the neck-trim stitches on the back.

⑥ Cast on and knit cuffs

Using smaller double-pointed needles, cast on ____ **cuff stitches**. Place a marker, join, and begin knitting in the round, using the same pattern stitch as you used for the welts and the neck trim.

⑦ Work sleeve increases

When cuffs are 1 inch (2.5 cm) long or desired length, change to larger double-pointed needles and begin pattern stitches, purling 1 stitch on each side of the marker to create a 2-stitch purled underarm "seam."

Work all rows of the triangle pattern, and then switch to the large check pattern (or use the pattern stitches of your choice).

Remember to center your stitch patterns (see pages 33 to 34).

AT THE SAME TIME, begin increasing for the sleeve as follows: On every 6th round, purl 1, increase 1, work in pattern to the next purl stitch, increase 1, purl 1.

Note: Remember, this sweater is designed to have a very loose cuff. If you've chosen to start with a more fitted cuff instead, you will need to start by working the increases on every 4th round.

Change to the 16-inch circular needle when the stitches no longer fit comfortably on the double-pointed needles.

Keep an eye on the shape of your sleeve and measure it against your model sweater or try your sleeve on after every few inches (cm) to make sure it is increasing in size at a comfortable rate. If your sleeve is becoming wide too quickly, start increasing every 8th round (every 6th round for fitted cuff). If it is not widening quickly enough, start increasing every 4th round (every 3rd round for fitted cuff).

Continue increasing until you reach _____ **sleeve stitches**. Work even until sleeve is _____ inches (cm) long (**sleeve length**).

Bind off loosely in pattern.

Make second sleeve the same way as the first, steps 6 and 7.

⑧ Finishing

Sew the sleeves into the armholes.

Weave in the ends.

Fitted Pullover with All-Over Pattern

My sample fitted pullover, modeled on the Danish nat-
trøjer, uses a large all-over pattern, but you can use a
smaller pattern if you prefer. This sweater is narrow at
the waist and increases at the sides to fit the bust. If you
make a sweater with a snug fit, you can add half-gussets
at the underarms to give yourself more room to move. If
you make a loose sweater, you can skip the half-gussets.

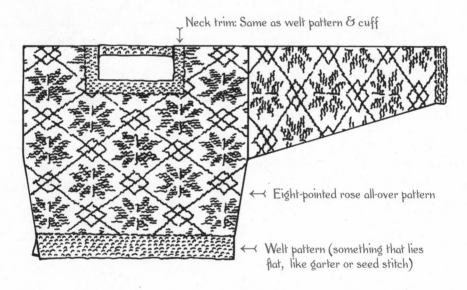

Neck trim: Same as welt pattern & cuff

←← Eight-pointed rose all-over pattern

←← Welt pattern (something that lies
flat, like garter or seed stitch)

✧ Texture pattern: all-over—choose a complex or easy main pattern

✧ Lower body worked in the round, with bottom welts,
    and upper body sections worked back and forth

✧ Fitted waist-length body and wide sleeves; optional half-gussets at underarms

✧ Shallow square neckline, with finishing trim knitted all-in-one with body

✧ Sleeves knitted from texture-stitch lower edge to shoulder and sewn on

The illustrations above and opposite show a sweater with a 40-inch (101.6-cm) bust circumference

and 18-inch (46-cm) body length (including 2 inches [5 cm] of welt) in worsted-weight yarn with

5 stitches and 7 rows to the inch (20 stitches and 28 rows to 10 cm).

Get ready   *yarn & needles*

Yarn

Select a smooth, tightly twisted yarn to make sure the pattern stitches will pop.

The patterns will be most visible if you use light-colored yarn. Red, blue, and green were the most popular colors for Danish *nattrøjer*, but any light to medium color will be beautiful. Dark colors will also be gorgeous, but they will make it much harder to see your stitches—and to follow the charts while you are working. If you are not sure the stitches will show up adequately, buy one ball of yarn and make a swatch.

Any weight of yarn will work, but for practice I suggest a medium-weight yarn and U.S. size 7 or 8 (4.5 or 5 mm) knitting needles. For a traditional sweater, select a lighter weight yarn.

Needle guidelines are on page 22. See the yarn estimate table on page 23 for yardages.

Knitting needles

In a size appropriate for the yarn you've chosen:

✧ Circular needle for body: for most adult sweaters, you will want a needle at least 29 inches (74 cm) long

✧ Circular needle for sleeves: 16 inches (40 cm) long

✧ Double-pointed needles for lower sleeves: set of 4 or 5

Two sizes smaller than primary needles:

✧ Straight needle or circular needle for welts: if you use a circular needle, it should be at least 16 inches (40 cm) long

✧ Double-pointed needles for cuffs: set of 4 or 5

Get set *stitches, gauge & size*	Denmark Fitted Pullover

Stitches and gauge

① Select pattern stitches for your sweater. Use the stitches shown in the illustration on pages 92 and 93 or choose your own combination of knit-and-purl pattern stitches.

② Make a gauge swatch in your main pattern stitch.

③ Measure your gauge. Write the stitch gauge and row gauge on the sweater-planning worksheet on page 97.

The texture patterns inspired by sweaters from Denmark are on pages 73 through 75; the large rose all-over pattern is on page 75.

Size

① Measure your favorite sweater or use the size charts on page 16 to determine the basic dimensions for your sweater. Write the measurements on the visual plan on page 96 and the sweater-planning worksheet on page 97.

② Measure your waist and add ease (see the ease chart on page 15) or measure the waist of your favorite *fitted* sweater.

③ Use the calculations on the worksheets on pages 97 and 98 to figure all the remaining numbers before you start, or just calculate each new number as you need it.

④ Transfer the resulting numbers to the visual plan on page 96 or the step-by-step instructions on pages 99 to 101, depending on how much guiding detail you would like to have while you knit.

Knit! *option I: using a visual plan*

Denmark
Fitted Pullover

For knitters who are ready to work from the basic concept

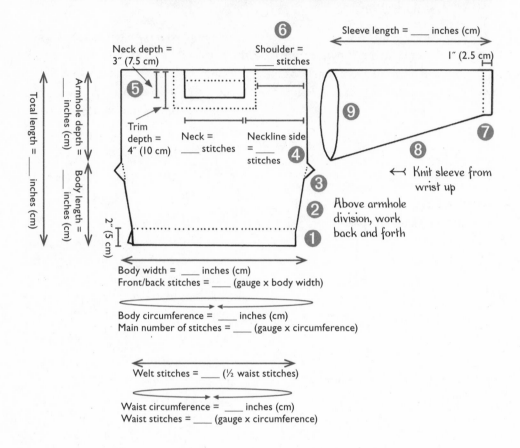

Neck depth = 3″ (7.5 cm)

Shoulder = ____ stitches

⑥

Sleeve length = ____ inches (cm)

1″ (2.5 cm)

Total length = ____ inches (cm)

Armhole depth = ____ inches (cm)

Body length = ____ inches (cm)

⑤

Trim depth = 4″ (10 cm)

Neck = ____ stitches

Neckline side = ____ stitches

④

⑨

⑧

⑦

← Knit sleeve from wrist up

③

② Above armhole division, work back and forth

①

2″ (5 cm)

Body width = ____ inches (cm)
Front/back stitches = ____ (gauge x body width)

Body circumference = ____ inches (cm)
Main number of stitches = ____ (gauge x circumference)

Welt stitches = ____ (½ waist stitches)

Waist circumference = ____ inches (cm)
Waist stitches = ____ (gauge x circumference)

BODY

① Cast on ____ stitches (welt stitches) and knit welts; join

② Work lower body, increasing at sides to ____ stitches (main number of stitches)

③ Work half-gussets (optional)

④ Separate for upper back and upper front

⑤ Work neck trim (____ neck trim stitches each side) and opening: ____ stitches

⑥ Join shoulders: ____ stitches

SLEEVES

⑦ Cast on ____ stitches and knit cuffs

⑧ Increase to ____ sleeve stitches

⑨ Sew in sleeves

Knit! option 2: using planning worksheets
Denmark
Fitted Pullover

For knitters who want to plan thoroughly in advance

Measurements

	Calculation	Example	Description
Stitch gauge	____ stitches = 1 inch or 1 cm	**5** stitches = 1 inch	**Stitch gauge** is critical for knitting a sweater that fits properly.
Row gauge	____ rows = 1 inch or 1 cm	**6** rows = 1 inch	**Row gauge** is not critical for this sweater.
Body width at underarm	____ inches (cm)	**20** inches	Measure the **width** of the sweater body.
Body circumference	____ x 2 = ____	20 x 2 = **40** inches	Double the body width for the **circumference of the sweater**.
Waist circumference	____ inches (cm)	**34** inches	Measure your **waist** or your favorite sweater. *See page 95, Size, item 2.*
Total length	____ inches (cm)	**18** inches	Measure the **length** of the sweater body, or use back waist length, which is measured from the most prominent bone at the back of the neck to the waistline, and add between 1 and 3 inches (2.5 and 7.5 cm) to cover waistline, if desired.
Sleeve length	____ inches (cm)	**18** inches	Measure the **sleeve length** from wrist to underarm.
Armhole depth	____ ÷ 4 = ____	40 ÷ 4 = **10** inches	Divide the body circumference by 4 to calculate the **armhole depth**.
Body length	____ − ____ = ____	18 − 10 = **8** inches	Subtract the armhole depth from the total body length to calculate the **length of the body from the cast-on edge to the armhole**.
Sleeve circumference	____ x 2 = ____	10 x 2 = **20** inches	Double the armhole depth for the **circumference of the sleeve**.

This example has been set up with numbers that clearly demonstrate the simple calculations. Those numbers happen to result in an adult's sweater with a finished chest measurement of 40″ (102 cm) that falls to just below the waistline. If you're not that size, and only a few of us will be, use the guidelines on pages 14 through 16 and measurements you gather for yourself to make a sweater that is customized for its wearer.

Stitch counts

		Calculation	Example	Description
a	Main number of stitches	___ x ___ = ___	40 x 5 = **200**	Multiply the body circumference by your stitch gauge to calculate the **main number of stitches**.
	Waist stitches	___ x ___ = ___	34 x 5 = **170**	Multiply the waist measurement (including ease) by your stitch gauge to calculate the **number of waist stitches**.
b	Welt stitches	___ ÷ 2 = ___	170 ÷ 2 = **85**	Divide the number of waist stitches in half to calculate the **number of stitches to cast on for each welt**. Round off to the nearest multiple of the welt pattern stitch, if necessary. *See tip on the next page.*
	Upper front & Upper back stitches	___ ÷ 2 = ___	200 ÷ 2 = **100**	Divide the main number of stitches in half to calculate the **number of stitches in the upper front and upper back**.
c	Neck stitches & Shoulder stitches	___ ÷ 3 = ___	100 ÷ 3 = **33** **33** stitches for each shoulder, **34** stitches for neck	Divide the number of stitches in the upper front in thirds to calculate the **number of stitches in the neck and shoulders**. If your number of stitches is not a multiple of 3, include the extra stitches with the neck. Make sure you have the same number of stitches in each shoulder.
d	Neck trim stitches	___ + ___ = ___	10 + 34 = **44**	Add 2 inches' (5 cm) worth of stitches to the number of stitches in the neck. This is the **number of stitches in your neck trim**.
e	Neck side stitches	___ − ___ = ___ ___ ÷ 2 = ___	100 − 44 = **56** 56 ÷ 2 = **28**	Subtract the number of stitches in your neck trim from the number of stitches for the front. If this is an odd number, decrease 1 stitch. Divide the result in half to calculate the **neck side stitches** (to center the neckline).
f	Sleeve stitches	___ x ___ = ___	20 x 5 = **100**	Multiply the sleeve circumference by your stitch gauge to calculate the **number of sleeve stitches** needed at the top of the sleeve. *Note:* If you are working half-gussets, add the number of stitches at the top of the half-gusset to this total.
g	Cuff stitches	___	**60**	After you knit the body of your sweater, wrap the ribbing very loosely around your wrist and count the **number of stitches for the cuff**. This sweater is meant to have a very loose-fitting cuff.

Need a slightly different stitch count? Increase or decrease by a few.

Knit! *option 3: a step-by-step project sheet*

Denmark
Fitted Pullover

For knitters who would like detailed instructions

Use this project sheet if you are not yet comfortable working directly from the sweater-planning diagram. With time, you'll find that you no longer need to refer to these instructions.

Do the calculations on the planning worksheets on pages 97 and 98 so you have the numbers to fill in here.

❶ Cast on and knit welts

With the smaller 29-inch (74-cm) circular needle, cast on ____ stitches (**welt stitches;** see tip below).

Work in 2x2 check stitch or the pattern stitch of your choice until the welt measures 2 inches (5 cm).

Make a second welt to match the first.

Join welts to begin working in the round (see technique on page 71).

❷ Work lower body

Change to the larger circular needle and eight-point rose pattern stitch (page 75). On the next round, when you reach the 2 purl "seam" stitches at the first join of the welt sections, purl these 2 overlapped stitches. Knit across the first welt section. Purl the 2 overlapped stitches at the second join of the welt sections, on the other side of the sweater. Knit across the second welt section. You now have 2 purl stitches marking each side "seam" of the sweater.

Begin to work the eight-point rose pattern or the pattern stitch of your choice, continuing to purl the 2 stitches at each side.

Remember to center your stitch patterns (see pages 33 to 34).

AT THE SAME TIME, increase 1 stitch before and after the purl "seams" every 6th round. Keep an eye on the shape of your body to make sure it is increasing at a comfortable rate. You need to increase to ____ stitches (**main number of stitches**) before you reach ____ inches (**body length**). If your body is becoming wide too quickly, start increasing every 8th round. If it is not widening quickly enough, start increasing every 4th round.

Continue increasing until you have ____ stitches (**main number of stitches**).

If you are not adding the optional half-gussets, work even until the body measures ____ inches (cm) (**body length**) from the cast-on edge.

~~~~~~~~~~~~~~~~

Tip: Welts are often worked in a pattern stitch that spreads out a bit, like garter stitch. One way to compensate for this is to work the welts on smaller-sized needles, as described here. Another is to cast on slightly fewer stitches. Start with smaller needles and the number of stitches specified. Adjust if necessary to accommodate your choice of welt patterns. Remember that when you join the two welt sections you will "lose" 4 stitches.

99

If you want a little extra wiggle-room for arm movement in your sweater, add the optional half-gussets: Using the technique described on page 72, work underarm half-gussets when the sweater measures 1 inch (2.5 cm) less than **body length** (____ inches [cm]), or ____ inches (cm).

❸ Separate for upper back and upper front

You will work the upper back and upper front back and forth on the larger circular needle, with half the stitches on hold as you work each section. (Place the stitches that are on hold on a piece of scrap yarn or a large stitch holder.)

If you worked half-gussets, bind off the half-gusset stitches between the purl stitches.

Separate the knitting into front and back, placing the separation points at each side between the 2 purl stitches. Each section should have 1 purl stitch on each end. Put one section on hold for the front, and leave the remaining stitches on the needle to work the upper back.

Upper back, including neckline trim

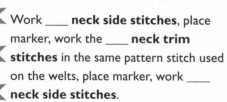

Work back and forth in pattern until the back of the sweater measures 1 inch (2.5 cm) less than **total length** (____ inches [cm]), or ____ inches (cm).

Work ____ **neck side stitches**, place marker, work the ____ **neck trim stitches** in the same pattern stitch used on the welts, place marker, work ____ **neck side stitches**.

Work the pattern as established, slipping

markers when you come to them. When the back measures ____ inches (cm) (**total length**), bind off the center back ____ **neck stitches**, making sure you have the same number of stitches on each shoulder and in the neckline trim on each side of the neck. Place these shoulder and neck-trim stitches on hold.

Upper front

Put the upper-front stitches back on the needle. Join the yarn at the right edge of the front and work back and forth in pattern as established until the front measures 4 inches (10 cm) less than **total length** (____ inches [cm]), or ____ inches (cm).

❹ Shape neckline on upper front

Begin the neck trim as for the back and work until the trim measures 1 inch (2.5 cm). The front should be 3 inches (7.5 cm) shorter than the back. Bind off the center front ____ **neck stitches**, making sure you have the same number of stitches on each shoulder and in the neck trim on each side of the neck. These numbers also need to match the number of stitches on hold for the back.

Work each of the 2 shoulders separately in pattern as established until the front is as long as the back.

❺ Join shoulders

Join the front and back at each shoulder using the three-needle bind-off. The neck-trim stitches on the front should line up with the neck-trim stitches on the back.

6 Cast on and knit cuffs

Using smaller double-pointed needles, cast on _____ **cuff stitches.** Place a marker, join, and begin knitting in the round, using the same pattern stitch as you used for the welts and the neck trim.

7 Work sleeve increases

When cuffs are 1 inch (2.5 cm) long or desired length, change to larger double-pointed needles and begin the all-over pattern stitch of your choice, purling 1 stitch on each side of the marker to create a 2-stitch purled underarm "seam."

Remember to center your stitch patterns (see pages 33 to 34).

AT THE SAME TIME, begin increasing for the sleeve as follows: On every 6th round, purl 1, increase 1, work in pattern to the next purl stitch, increase 1, purl 1.

Note: Remember, this sweater is designed to have a very loose cuff. If you've chosen to start with a fitted cuff instead, you will need to start by working the increases on every 4th round.

Change to the 16-inch circular needle when the stitches no longer fit comfortably on the double-pointed needles.

Keep an eye on the shape of your sleeve and measure it against your model sweater or try your sweater on after every few inches (cm) to make sure the sleeve is increasing at a comfortable rate. If your sleeve is becoming wide too quickly, start increasing every 8th round (6th round for narrow cuff). If it is not widening quickly enough, start increasing every 4th round (3rd round for narrow cuff).

Continue increasing until you have _____ **sleeve stitches.** Work even until the sleeve is _____ inches (cm) long (**sleeve length**).

If you are working half-gussets, the upper sleeve will be wider by the number of stitches at the top of the half-gusset (_____ **sleeve stitches** plus half-gusset stitches = _____ upper sleeve stitches). If you are working half-gussets, you may want to increase more rapidly within the final 1 inch (2.5 cm) of the sleeve length—experiment to discover the increase combination that looks like it will work best for the body shape of the sweater's intended wearer.

Bind off loosely in pattern.

Make second sleeve the same way as the first, steps 6 and 7.

8 Finishing

Sew the sleeves into the armholes.

Weave in the ends.

Norway

Knitting came late to Norway, probably in the mid-1800s. Yet one of the most famous sweater designs of all times is the Norwegian *lusekofte* (lice jacket). Named for the simple *luse*, or "louse," color pattern that covers the main portion of the body, these sweaters, which come from the rural Setesdal valley, are recognized around the world.

The lice pattern, created with white stitches scattered over a black background, was originally made with the tiny flecks on every other round, forming a dense, heavy fabric appropriate for wear in the cold Scandinavian climate. Today, the lice are knitted on every fourth round, producing a softer, lighter fabric.

It is impossible to know exactly when and where the lice pattern originated. It may have first appeared when knitters tucked loose fleece or pile into the stitches for mitten fabrics, to add warmth. Small pieces of the added wool may have shown on the outsides of the mittens, inspiring a new design in color knitting.

This world-famous Norwegian sweater style originated in the Setesdal valley at a time when the people of that area lived a nomadic lifestyle. Their winter homes were quite dark, and most knitting was done during the summer, when they moved to mountain farms. At the latitude where they lived, near the arctic circle, summer evenings were long and light-filled, and provided ample knitting time.

The *lusekofte* was originally a man's garment, with a wide white band at the lower edge that was tucked into high-waisted trousers. Having the white portion show was tantamount to having your underwear exposed. Although young people today seem to have no problem with this type of fashion statement, it was quite an embarrassment in the past. The main body of the sweater was knitted with white patterns on a black background, perhaps to hide soot from cooking and heating fires in an environment where washing clothes in the winter was difficult.

These Norwegian-style sweaters have bands of color patterning. They are knitted in the round to the shoulder, and the armholes are cut open—a relatively modern technique.

Traditionally, each sweater was unique and the knitters did not write down their patterns. Each knitter strove for originality and designed on the needles, choosing a new pattern stitch after completing the previous one. Although some pattern elements were commonly used, such as the lice pattern and the Saint Andrew's cross, knitters valued fresh ideas and would not copy other knitters' sweaters.

The sweaters have always been knitted in the round. This technique makes the pattern easier to knit because the right side is always showing. In addition, one-piece circular sweaters were more portable than sweaters made in pieces. Until circular needles were introduced, Norwegian knitters used long double-pointed needles. The live stitches were arranged on four needles and a fifth was used to work the stitches. Circular needles first appeared in Norway in 1881, although they didn't start to catch on until around 1925.

Chapter

5

CHAPTER HIGHLIGHTS

Skills

✓ Two-color patterning worked in the round

Techniques

✓ Modern cut armholes

✓ Simple faced boat neck or cut-opening crew neck

Garment styling

✓ Drop shoulder, standard pullover style—boat neck, turtleneck, crew neck

✓ Upper body sections worked in the round

✓ Sleeves knitted from cuff to shoulder and sewn on, with facings

Lusekofte sweaters were started at the hem and worked upward to the shoulders. After the body was completed, the fabric was cut open to form the armholes. Then the shoulders were joined. The sleeves were traditionally picked up and knitted down to the cuffs. After the sweater parts had been completed, the neckline was cut open. Intricately embroidered trim was then added to the neck and cuffs. Often a fabric facing was also sewn inside the neck area, running from shoulder to shoulder. This facing added warmth, covered the cut edges of the fabric, and possibly acted as a form of shoulder pads.

Today, the sleeves on Norwegian sweaters are often made separately, worked from the cuff up, and then sewn into the armholes. A few extra rows are knitted at the top of the sleeve to form a facing that encases the cut edge of the armhole. At the neckline, the sweaters are often finished off with a self-facing, instead of the embroidered trim.

Techniques

Knitting with two colors

Knitting with two colors in a single row to form color patterns that reach all the way across your knitting is called Fair Isle, Jacquard, or stranded knitting. There are several ways to hold the yarn when knitting with multiple colors.

You can hold both colors in the same hand. This is easier to do when you knit Continental-style, because you can just "pick" off the color you need. If you are holding both colors in one hand, make sure you always take the main color over the top of the contrasting color and take the contrasting color under the main color, so the strands do not twist.

I prefer to hold one color in my right hand and the other in my left.

Working with both hands, hold the main color in your right hand (English style) and the contrasting color in your left hand (Continental style). Strand the unused color loosely across the back of the work.

If you have more than 5 stitches of the background color, weave in the contrasting color to avoid inordinately long floats: The technique I'll describe is based on my preferred method of holding one yarn in each hand, with the most frequently used color in the right hand.

    I. Lift the index finger of your left hand to lift the lefthand yarn *above* the working yarn. Knit one stitch.

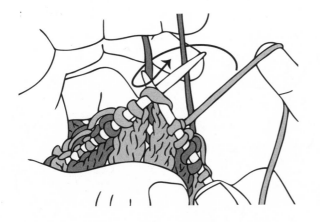

Lift the lefthand yarn above the working yarn and knit one stitch.

    2. Move the yarn in your left hand *below* the working yarn. Knit the next stitch as usual.

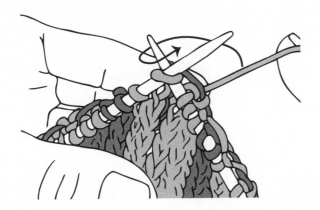

Then drop the lefthand yarn below the working yarn and knit one stitch.

Embroidered trim

Embroidered trim has been traditionally used on Norwegian sweaters. On the necklines and cuffs of the sweaters that follow, I have used knitted trims. If you want to add embroidered trim to your sweaters, check out the books on Norwegian knitting in the bibliography for ideas and instructions.

Pattern stitches

Stripes

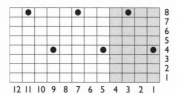

Repeat: I stitch by 2 rows

Lice

Repeat: 4 stitches (plus 2 to balance) by 8 rows

Dark on light (above right) and
light on dark (below right)

Zigzag

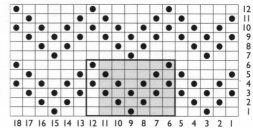

Repeat: 6 stitches (plus I to balance) by 6 rows

Saint Andrew's cross

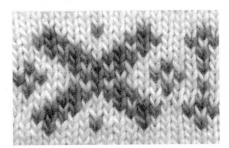

Repeat: 18 stitches (plus 3—repeat stitches 1, 2, and 3—to balance) by 13 rows

Snowflake

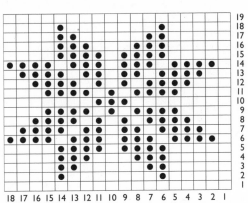

Repeat: 18 stitches (plus 1 to balance) by 19 rows

Diamonds

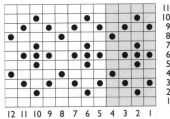

Repeat: 4 stitches (plus 1 to balance) by 11 rows

Headband

This headband is a quick knit that will provide an introduction to knitting with two colors. Each headband offers practice working with one pattern stitch. If you make a headband in each pattern you plan to use in your sweater, you will have all the stitch patterns memorized—and a headband for every day of the week.

← Lice

↑ Stripes and diamonds

← Snowflakes

✓ Color patterning worked in the round

These illustrations show headbands that are 20 inches (51-cm) in circumference and about 4 inches (10 cm) wide in worsted-weight yarn with 5 stitches and about 6 or 7 rows to the inch (20 stitches and 24 to 28 rows to 10 cm).

Get ready   *yarn & needle*

Norway
Headband

Yarn

Smooth yarn will show off the stitches and color patterns best, making it easy to keep track of where you are on the chart.

Any weight of yarn will work, but for practice I suggest a medium-weight yarn and U.S. size 7 or 8 (4.5 or 5 mm) knitting needles. Approximately 50 yards (46 m) of each color will be ample for making a headband.

Knitting needle

In a size appropriate for the yarn you've chosen:

✧ Circular needle: 16 inches (40 cm) long

Needle guidelines are on page 22.

Get set *stitches, gauge & size*

Stitches and gauge

① Select the stitch for your headband. Use a pattern shown on the sample illustration, or choose your favorite from the other charts on pages 106 and 107.

② Make a gauge swatch in the pattern stitch you have chosen.

③ Measure your stitch gauge. Write it on the planning worksheet on page III.

Size

① Select a size for your headband and write the measurements in the boxes on the planning worksheet on page III. These headbands fit snugly. If you want a looser band, add 1 or 2 inches (a few centimeters) to the circumference.

② Use the calculations on the worksheet to figure the remaining numbers.

③ Transfer the numbers to the visual plan below or the step-by-step instructions on page III, depending on how much guiding detail you would like to have while you knit.

⁂ Child: 16-inch (40.6-cm) circumference

⁂ Adult medium: 18-inch (45.7-cm) circumference

⁂ Adult large: 20-inch (50.8-cm) circumference

Knit! *option I: using a visual plan*

For knitters who are ready to work from the basic concept

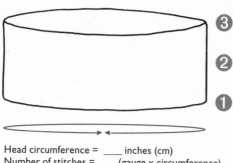

Head circumference = ____ inches (cm)
Number of stitches = ____ (gauge x circumference)

1 Cast on ____ stitches
2 Knit pattern stitches
3 Bind off and finish

Knit!   *option 2: using a planning worksheet*   Norway Headband

For knitters who want to plan thoroughly in advance

Measurements and stitch counts

	Calculation	Example	Description
Stitch gauge	____ stitches = 1 inch or 1 cm	**5** stitches = 1 inch	**Stitch gauge** is critical for knitting a headband that fits properly.
Circumference	____ inches (cm)	**20** inches	Desired **circumference** of headband.
Main number of stitches	____ x ____ = ____	20 x 5 = **100** stitches	Multiply the circumference by your stitch gauge to calculate the **number of stitches**. Remember to center your stitch pattern or round the stitch count up or down as necessary (see pages 33 to 34).

Need a slightly different stitch count? Increase or decrease by a few.

Knit!   *option 3: a step-by-step project sheet*   Norway Headband

For knitters who would like detailed instructions

Do the calculations on the planning worksheet above so you have the numbers to fill in here.

❶ Cast on

Cast on ____ stitches (**main number of stitches**). Join, being careful not to twist, and knit in the round.

❷ Knit the headband

Work entire chart of chosen pattern once or twice, until headband is the desired width.

❸ Finishing

Bind off.

Weave in the ends.

If you like, you can line the headband with fleece fabric.

Technical note: As alternatives to the fleece fabric lining, you can leave the headband as is (the edges will curl forward slightly) or you can work a few rows of a non-rolling stitch (like garter stitch or seed stitch) after the cast-on and before the bind-off.

Boatneck Sweater with Optional Turtleneck

This garment has the easiest neckline of any sweater in this collection. It requires absolutely no shaping. The neck is left open when the shoulders are sewn together, and a facing is tacked down to make the neckline lie flat.

Use black and white for a traditional design, with a few red stripes for a splash of color. For a more colorful sweater, try another dark or rich color with pattern stitches in white or off-white. Or experiment with a self-striping yarn for the contrasting color and a solid for the main color.

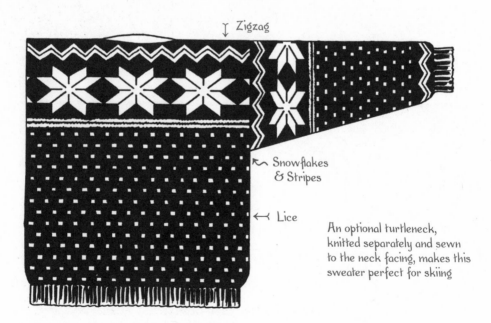

⅃ Zigzag

⤷ Snowflakes & Stripes

↢ Lice

An optional turtleneck, knitted separately and sewn to the neck facing, makes this sweater perfect for skiing

✓ Color patterning: in horizontal bands

✓ Worked in the round, with modern-style, cut armholes

✓ Very simple neckline

✓ Sleeves worked from cuffs up to facings and sewn into place

The sweater on the right has been designed in worsted-weight yarn with 5 stitches and 6 rows to the inch (20 stitches and 24 rows to 10 cm). The sweater on the left (and opposite) is in chunky-weight yarn with 3 stitches and 4 rows to the inch (12 stitches and 16 rows to 10 cm). Both sweaters have a 40-inch (101.6-cm) body circumference and 24-inch (61-cm) body length (including 2 inches [5 cm] of ribbing). There are extra plain rows between the design bands to put the patterns where the knitter wants them.

Get ready   *how to design your sweater*

Yarn

Wool yarn works best for knitting that will be cut open, but any animal fiber or wool-blend yarn is also appropriate. If you've never cut your knitting before, don't try working with cotton or any other slippery yarn.

Any weight of yarn will work, but for practice I suggest a lightweight yarn and U.S. size 5 or 6 (3.75 or 4 mm) knitting needles. Because you are using two colors throughout, the knitting will be significantly heavier than when you work with a single color.

*Needle guidelines are on page 22.
See the yarn estimate table on page
23 for yardages.*

Knitting needles

In a size appropriate for the yarn you've chosen:

✧ Circular needle for body: for most adult sweaters, you will want a needle at least 29 inches (74 cm) long

✧ Circular needle for upper sleeves and neckband: 16 inches (40 cm) long

✧ Double-pointed needles for lower sleeves: set of 4 or 5

Optional for ribbings: Two sizes smaller than primary needles:

✧ Circular needle for body ribbing: for most adult sweaters, you will want a needle at least 29 inches (74 cm) long

✧ Double-pointed needles for cuffs: set of 4 or 5

✧ Optional circular needle (for turtleneck): 16 inches (40 cm) long; the turtleneck can also be knitted on double-pointed needles

If you decide to use smaller needles for the ribbings, I'll count on you to know when to switch between needle sizes. Everyone else: Work on same-size needles with me. You'll do fine.

Get set *stitches, gauge & size*	Norway
	Boatneck Sweater

Stitches and gauge

① Select pattern stitches for your sweater. Use the combination shown in the illustrations on pages 112 and 113 or choose your own combination of stitches. You may use different pattern stitches, or use one or two pattern stitches repeatedly.

② Make a gauge swatch in stockinette stitch using the lice chart and two-color knitting.

③ Measure your gauge. Write the stitch gauge and row gauge on the sweater-planning worksheet on page 117.

④ Knit a swatch of each pattern stitch you will be using and measure the height of each pattern stitch. (Alternatively, you can use the row gauge to calculate the height of each chart.) *See technical note below.*

Size

① Measure your favorite sweater or use the size charts on page 16 to determine the basic dimensions for your sweater. Write the measurements on the visual plan on page 116 and the sweater-planning worksheet on page 117.

② Use the calculations on the worksheets on pages 117 and 118 to figure all the remaining numbers before you start, or just calculate each new number as you need it.

③ Transfer the resulting numbers to the visual plan on page 116 or the step-by-step instructions 119 and 120, depending on how much guiding detail you would like to have while you knit.

> The color patterns inspired by sweaters from Norway are on pages 106 and 107.

Technical note: Although row gauge is not critical in this sweater, knowing the total height of all your chosen pattern stitches lets you check to be sure they will fit within the length of the sweater body.

In addition, if your rows are very tall or very short, the pattern stitches may look distorted. You can troubleshoot this by knitting the swatches.

If you prefer, you can choose your pattern stitches as you go along and wing it, in which case you may not be able to complete the chart for the pattern at the shoulders. If it looks like you won't have enough room for a larger pattern in the allotted space, work the small diamonds or stripes here. If you are going to wing it, I trust that you can make the necessary adjustments!

Knit! *option I: using a visual plan*

Norway
Boatneck Sweater

For knitters who are ready to work from the basic concept

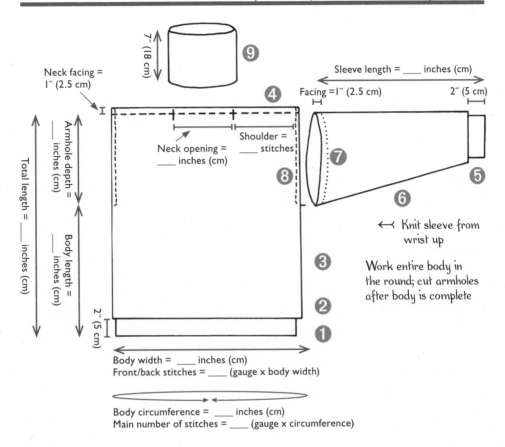

7″ (18 cm)

⑨

Neck facing =
1″ (2.5 cm)

Sleeve length = ____ inches (cm)

Facing = 1″ (2.5 cm)   2″ (5 cm)

④

Armhole depth = ____ inches (cm)

I

Neck opening = ____ inches (cm)

Shoulder = ____ stitches

⑧

⑦

⑤

⑥

Total length = ____ inches (cm)

Body length = ____ inches (cm)

③

← Knit sleeve from wrist up

Work entire body in the round; cut armholes after body is complete

②

2″ (5 cm)

①

Body width = ____ inches (cm)
Front/back stitches = ____ (gauge x body width)

Body circumference = ____ inches (cm)
Main number of stitches = ____ (gauge x circumference)

BODY

❶ Cast on ____ stitches (90% of main number of stitches) and knit ribbing

❷ Increase to ____ stitches (main number of stitches), change to stockinette stitch and lice pattern, and work lower body

❸ Work patterns to desired length

❹ Work neck facing

SLEEVES

❺ Cast on ____ cuff stitches and knit ribbing

❻ Increase to ____ sleeve stitches

❼ Knit armhole facing and bind off

FINISH

❽ Cut armholes open, sew shoulder seams, sew sleeves into armholes, and hem facings

OPTIONAL TURTLENECK

❾ Cast on ____ turtleneck stitches; knit turtleneck and sew in place

Knit! *option 2: using planning worksheets*

Norway
Boatneck Sweater

For knitters who want to plan thoroughly in advance

Measurements

	Calculation	Example	Description
Stitch gauge	____ stitches = 1 inch or 1 cm	**5** stitches = 1 inch	**Stitch gauge** is critical for knitting a sweater that fits properly.
Row gauge	____ rows = 1 inch or 1 cm	**6** rows = 1 inch	**Row gauge** is not critical for this sweater. *But see technical note on page 115.*
Body width	____ inches (cm)	**20** inches	Measure the **width** of the sweater body.
Body circumference	___ x 2 = ____	**40** inches	Double the body width for the **circumference of the sweater**.
Total length	____ inches (cm)	**24** inches	Measure the **length** of the sweater body.
Sleeve length	____ inches (cm)	**18** inches	Measure the **sleeve length** from wrist to underarm.
Armhole depth	___ ÷ 4 = ____	**40 ÷ 4 = 10** inches	Divide the body circumference by 4 to calculate the **armhole depth**.
Neck width	___ ÷ 3 = ____	**20 ÷ 3 = 6¾** inches	Measure the neck on your sample sweater, or divide the body width in thirds to determine the **width of the neck opening**.
Body length	___ – ___ = ___	**24 – 10 = 14** inches	Subtract the armhole depth from the total body length to calculate the **length of the body from the cast-on edge to the armhole**.
Sleeve circumference	___ x 2 = ____	**10 x 2 = 20** inches	Double the armhole depth for the **circumference of the sleeve**.
Height of patterns	___ + ___ + ___ + ___ = ___	**3 + 2 + 3 + 1 + 1 = 10** inches	Add together the **heights of all of your pattern stitches**.
Amount of lice pattern	___ – ___ = ___ ___ – 2 = ___	**24 – 10 = 14** inches **14 – 2 = 12** inches	Subtract the total height of all of your pattern stitches from the total body length. Subtract 2 inches (5 cm) to account for the ribbing at the bottom of the sweater. The result is the **amount of lice pattern** to knit directly above the ribbing. You can fudge this and just make it up as you go if you prefer.

A

B

C

D

E

Stitch counts

		Calculation	Example	Description
a	Main number of stitches	___ x ___ = ___	40 x 5 = **200**	Multiply the body circumference by your stitch gauge to calculate the **main number of stitches**.
b	90% of main number of stitches	___ x 0.9 = ___	200 x 0.9 = **180**	Take 90 percent of the main number of stitches to calculate the **number of stitches to cast on**. If this is an odd number, add 1 so you have an even number of stitches for working the k1, p1 ribbing.
c	Front stitches & Back stitches	___ ÷ 2 = ___	200 ÷ 2 = **100**	Divide the main number of stitches in half to determine the **number of stitches in the front and back**.
d	Sleeve stitches	___ x ___ = ___	20 x 5 = **100**	Multiply the sleeve circumference by your stitch gauge to calculate the **number of sleeve stitches** needed at the top of the sleeve.
e	Cuff stitches	___	**40**	After you knit the body of your sweater, wrap the ribbing around your wrist and count the **number of stitches for the cuff**. For a rough estimate of this number, divide the main number of stitches by 5.
f	Turtleneck stitches (optional)	___	**76**	After you knit the body of your sweater, wrap the ribbing around your neck and count the **number of stitches to cast on for the optional turtleneck**. The turtleneck will be a bit more than a third of the main number of stitches, because it is worked in ribbing, which draws in.

Need a slightly different stitch count? Increase or decrease by a few.

This example has been set up with numbers that clearly demonstrate the simple calculations. Those numbers happen to result in an adult's sweater with a finished chest measurement of 40″ (102 cm) that falls to a generous hip length. If you're not that size, and only a few of us will be, use the guidelines on pages 14 through 16 and measurements you gather for yourself to make a sweater that is customized for its wearer.

Knit! *option 3: a step-by-step project sheet*

Norway
Boatneck Sweater

For knitters who would like detailed instructions

Use this project sheet if you are not yet comfortable working directly from the sweater-planning diagram. With time, you'll find that you no longer need to refer to these instructions.

Do the calculations on the planning worksheets on pages 117 and 118 so you have the numbers to fill in here.

❶ Cast on and knit ribbing

 With the 29-inch (74-cm) circular needle, cast on ____ stitches (**90% of main number of stitches**). Join, being careful not to twist, place a marker at the beginning of the round, and knit in the round.

Work in k1, p1 ribbing until body measures 2 inches (5 cm), or until ribbing is desired length.

❷ Work lice pattern

 Change to stockinette stitch (knit every round) and lice pattern. Increase to ____ stitches (**main number of stitches**) on the first round as follows: *K9, increase 1, repeat from * to end of round.

On the next round, knit ____ **back stitches**, place a second marker, knit to end of round. You now have a marker at the beginning of the round and a second marker halfway around, marking the side "seams" of the sweater.

Work even in stockinette stitch and lice pattern until the body measures ____

inches (cm) (**amount of lice pattern**) from the top of the ribbing. (Or work for the desired length if you are winging it and choosing pattern stitches as you go.)

❸ Work patterns

You will work the body straight to the shoulder and will machine stitch and cut the fabric at each side "seam" to form the armholes.

Note: Remember to center your stitch patterns or adjust the stitch count as necessary when you begin each new pattern (see pages 33 to 35), and work a full repeat of the pattern stitch of your choice.

Work patterns until the body measures ____ inches (cm) (**total length**) from the cast-on edge.

❹ Work neck facing

Cut contrasting color.

Purl 1 round (turning ridge).

Work 1 inch (2.5 cm) even in stockinette stitch with background color. Bind off and set body aside.

❺ Cast on and knit cuffs

With double-pointed needles, cast on ____ **cuff stitches**. Place a marker, join, and begin knitting k1, p1 ribbing in the round.

6 Begin sleeve increases

When cuffs are 2 inches (5 cm) long or desired length, change to pattern stitches of your choice. Usually sweaters in this style have one or two small pattern bands above the cuff, then a large section of lice pattern, followed by two or three pattern bands at the shoulder.

AT THE SAME TIME, begin increasing for the sleeve as follows: On every 4th round, knit 1, increase 1, work in pattern to the next purl stitch, increase 1, knit 1.

Change to a 16-inch (40-cm) circular needle when the stitches no longer fit comfortably on the double-pointed needles.

Keep an eye on the shape of your sleeve and measure it against your model sweater or try your sleeve on after every few inches (cm) to make sure the sleeve is increasing at a comfortable rate. If your sleeve is becoming wide too quickly, start increasing every 6th round. If it is not widening enough, start increasing every 3rd round.

Continue increasing until you have _____ **sleeve stitches** and then work even until the sleeve is _____ inches (cm) long (**sleeve length**).

7 Knit facing and bind off sleeve

Work reverse stockinette stitch (purl every round) for ½ inch (1.25 cm) for armhole facing. Bind off all stitches.

Make second sleeve the same way as the first, steps 5 through 7.

8 Finishing

At each side seam, measure **armhole depth** (_____ inches [cm]) down from the bound-off edge to mark the armhole. With a sewing machine, make 2 rows of stitches on each side of the stitch directly at the side "seam." At the bottom of this column of stitches, sew back and forth a few times to reinforce the edge. Cut the armhole open with sharp sewing shears, stopping 1 stitch above the bottom of the machine stitching.

Turn the neck facing to the inside and join both shoulder seams, sewing the purl turning ridges together and leaving _____ inches (cm) (**neck width**) open in the center for the neckline. Tack down the facings on the inside.

Sew the sleeves into the armholes. Tack down the sleeve-top facings, covering the cut edges of the armholes.

Weave in the ends.

9 Turtleneck (optional)

Using a 16-inch (40-cm) circular needle, cast on _____ **turtleneck stitches**.

Place a marker, join, and begin knitting k1, p1 ribbing in the round. Continue until neck piece measures 7 inches (18 cm). Bind off loosely in pattern.

Sew the bottom edge of the turtleneck to the bottom (cast-off edge) of the neck facing inside. Fold the turtleneck to the outside.

From traditional to fashionable. . . .

Hiking and skiing have long been favorite winter sports in Scandinavia. They became even more popular after the industrial revolution, when a health movement in Norway promoted an outdoor lifestyle that was the polar opposite of the dark, dirty existence of many factory workers who lived in cities.

At the same time, traditional Norwegian sweaters were commercialized and made by machine as part of a marketing campaign to promote Norway as a tourist destination. After Dale of Norway started producing sweaters for the Winter Olympics in 1956, the garments became synonymous with skiing and winter sports.

By the mid-twentieth century, the distinctive Norwegian sweaters were no longer relegated to traditional festivals in rural villages and towns. Instead they appeared at outdoor sporting events around the world. The transition from traditional conservative garment to modern fashion statement was complete.

Cover sweater story: Norwegian design   *by Debbie O'Neill*

I started by thinking about yarn. I knew that I didn't want it to be too heavy, because the stranded sections would be too warm. I settled on a DK-weight, 100% wool, machine washable. I chose to knit on a smaller needle than is usual for that yarn so the gauge resembles that of a sportweight yarn.

I decided how large I wanted my sweater to be by measuring a pullover that I like and then calculated roughly how many stitches I would need to work the body in the round. I selected the largest motif I wanted to use (the snowflake on page 107) and figured out how many repeats would fit.

You nearly always need to adjust your stitch count to fit your pattern into the size you want to make. I adjusted upward, because I prefer sweaters to be large rather than small and because it took fewer stitches to adjust up than down.

Next I chose my smaller motifs. I expanded the zigzag motif—mine is taller and wider than the chart on page 106—so its repeat would be compatible with the snowflake. I wanted my zigzag to stand out, so I filled in all of its peaks to make it look more solid.

Finally, I wanted more color in my sweater than purple and natural, so I decided to work the little fleur-de-lis motif in gold and green.

I constructed the sweater in the round and steeked the armholes and neck. I hemmed the lower edges of the body and sleeves, as well as the collar. I worked the insides of the hems on a smaller needle (they are also in a contrasting color), so the hems would lie flat. I worked one purl row where I turned each hem.

Crewneck Sweater

This crewneck sweater is decorated with more elaborate pattern stitches than the boatneck design. If you want to add a bit of color to the classic black-and-white pattern-ing, add some snowflakes or zigzags in red across the white portion at the bottom of the body.

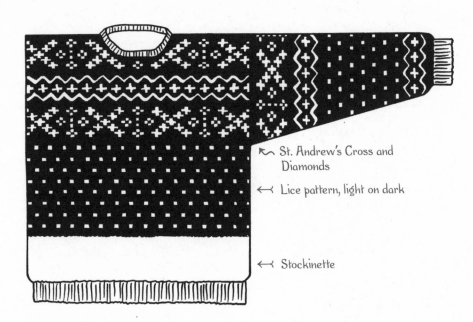

↖ St. Andrew's Cross and Diamonds

↞ Lice pattern, light on dark

↞ Stockinette

✔ Color patterning: all-over and in horizontal bands

✔ Worked in the round throughout, with modern-style, cut armholes

✔ Cut neckline finished with picked-up ribbing

✔ Sleeves worked from cuffs up to facings and sewn into place

The illustrations above and opposite show a sweater with a 40-inch (101.6-cm) body circumference and 24-inch (61-cm) body length (including 2 inches [5 cm] of ribbing) in chunky-weight yarn with 3 stitches and 4 rows to the inch (12 stitches and 16 rows to 10 cm).

Get ready *yarn & needles*

Yarn

Wool yarn works best for knitting that will be cut open, but any animal fiber or wool-blend yarn is also appropriate. If you've never cut your knitting before, don't try working with cotton or any other slippery yarn.

Any weight of yarn will work, but for practice I suggest a lightweight yarn and U.S. size 5 or 6 (3.75 or 4 mm) knitting needles. Because you are using two colors throughout, the knitting will be significantly heavier than when you work with a single color.

Needle guidelines are on page 22. See the yarn estimate table on page 23 for yardages.

Knitting needles

In a size appropriate for the yarn you've chosen:

✧ Circular needle for body: for most adult sweaters, you will want a needle at least 29 inches (74 cm) long

✧ Circular needle for upper sleeves: 16 inches (40 cm) long

✧ Double-pointed needles for lower sleeves: set of 4 or 5

Optional for ribbings: Two sizes smaller than primary needles:

✧ Circular needle for body ribbing: for most adult sweaters, you will want a needle at least 29 inches (74 cm) long

✧ Double-pointed needles for cuffs: set of 4 or 5

✧ Circular needle for neckband: 16 inches (40 cm) long (the neckband can also be worked on double-pointed needles used for cuffs)

If you decide to use smaller needles for the ribbings, I'll count on you to know when to switch between needle sizes. Everyone else: Work on same-size needles with me. You'll do fine.

| **Get set** *stitches, gauge & size* | Norway
Crewneck Sweater |

Stitches and gauge

① Select pattern stitches for your sweater. Use the combination shown in the illustrations on pages 122 and 123 or choose your own combination of stitches. You may use different pattern stitches, or repeat a small selection of stitches.

② Make a gauge swatch in your stockinette stitch using the lice chart and two-color knitting.

③ Measure your gauge. Write the stitch gauge and row gauge on the sweater-planning worksheet on page 127.

④ Knit a swatch of each pattern stitch you will be using and measure the height of each pattern stitch. (Alternatively, you can use the row gauge to calculate the height of each chart.) *See technical note below.*

Size

① Measure your favorite sweater or use the size charts on page 16 to determine the basic dimensions for your sweater. Write the measurements on the visual plan on page 126 and the sweater-planning worksheet on page 127.

② Use the calculations on the worksheets on pages 127 and 128 to figure all the remaining numbers before you start, or just calculate each new number as you need it.

③ Transfer the resulting numbers to the visual plan on page 126 or the step-by-step instructions on pages 129 to 131, depending on how much guiding detail you would like to have while you knit.

> The color patterns inspired by sweaters from Norway are on pages 106 and 107.

Technical note: Although row gauge is not critical in this sweater, knowing the total height of all your chosen pattern stitches lets you check to be sure they will fit within the length of the sweater body.

In addition, if your rows are very tall or very short, the pattern stitches may look distorted. You can troubleshoot this by knitting the swatches.

If you prefer, you can choose your pattern stitches as you go along and wing it, in which case you may not be able to complete the chart for the pattern at the shoulders. If it looks like you won't have enough room for a larger pattern in the allotted space, work the small diamonds or stripes here. If you are going to wing it, I trust that you can make the necessary adjustments!

Knit! *option I: using a visual plan*

Norway
Crewneck Sweater

For knitters who are ready to work from the basic concept

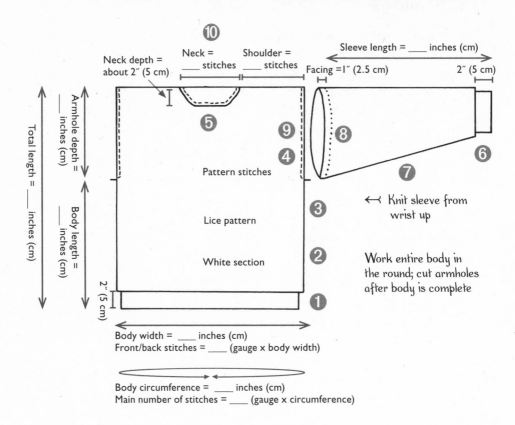

Neck depth = about 2″ (5 cm)

Neck = ____ stitches

Shoulder = ____ stitches

Sleeve length = ____ inches (cm)

Facing =1″ (2.5 cm)

2″ (5 cm)

Armhole depth = ____ inches (cm)

Total length = ____ inches (cm)

Body length = ____ inches (cm)

2″ (5 cm)

Pattern stitches

Lice pattern

White section

← Knit sleeve from wrist up

Work entire body in the round; cut armholes after body is complete

Body width = ____ inches (cm)
Front/back stitches = ____ (gauge x body width)

Body circumference = ____ inches (cm)
Main number of stitches = ____ (gauge x circumference)

BODY

❶ Cast on ____ stitches (90% of main number of stitches) and knit ribbing

❷ Increase to ____ stitches (main number of stitches) and work lower body

❸ Work white section, lice pattern, and pattern stitches to desired length

❹ Cut armholes open

❺ Cut neckline and join shoulders

SLEEVES

❻ Cast on ____ cuff stitches and knit ribbing

❼ Increase to ____ sleeve stitches

❽ Knit armhole facing and bind off

❾ Sew shoulder seams, sew sleeves into armholes, and hem facings

FINISH

❿ Work neckband

Knit! *option 2: using planning worksheets*

Norway
Crewneck Sweater

For knitters who want to plan thoroughly in advance

Measurements

	Calculation	Example	Description
Stitch gauge	____ stitches = 1 inch or 1 cm	**5** stitches = 1 inch	**Stitch gauge** is critical for knitting a sweater that fits properly.
Row gauge	____ rows = 1 inch or 1 cm	**6** rows = 1 inch	**Row gauge** is not critical for this sweater.
Body width	____ inches (cm)	**20** inches	Measure the **width** of the sweater body.
Body circumference	____ x 2 = ____	**40** inches	Double the body width for the **circumference of the sweater**.
Total length	____ inches (cm)	**24** inches	Measure the **length** of the sweater body.
Sleeve length	____ inches (cm)	**18** inches	Measure the **sleeve length** from wrist to underarm.
Armhole depth	____ ÷ 4 = ____	40 ÷ 4 = **10** inches	Divide the body circumference by 4 to calculate the **armhole depth**.
Body length	____ – ____ = ____	24 – 10 = **14** inches	Subtract the armhole depth from the total body length to calculate the **length of the body from the cast-on edge to the armhole**.
Sleeve circumference	____ x 2 = ____	10 x 2 = **20** inches	Double the armhole depth for the **circumference of the sleeve**.
Height of patterns	____ + ____ + ____ + ____ = ____	3 + 2 + 3 + 1 + 1 = **10** inches	Add together the **heights of all of your pattern stitches**.
Amount of white section plus lice pattern	____ – ____ = ____	24 – 10 = **14** inches	Subtract the total height of all of your pattern stitches from the total body length.
	____ – 2 = ____	14 – 2 = **12** inches	Subtract 2 inches (5 cm) to account for the ribbing at the bottom of the sweater. The result is the **amount of white section and lice pattern** to knit directly above the ribbing. Decide how much to knit in white and how much in the lice pattern. You can fudge this and just make it up as you go if you prefer.

A
B
C
D

127

Stitch counts

		Calculation	Example	Description
a	Main number of stitches	___ x ___ = ___	40 x 5 = **200**	Multiply the body circumference by your stitch gauge to calculate the **main number of stitches**.
b	90% of main number of stitches	___ x 0.9 = ___	200 x 0.9 = **180**	Take 90 percent of the main number of stitches to calculate the **number of stitches to cast on**. If this is an odd number, add 1 so you have an even number of stitches for working the k1, p1 ribbing.
c	Front stitches & Back stitches	___ ÷ 2 = ___	200 ÷ 2 = **100**	Divide the main number of stitches in half to determine the **number of stitches in the front and back**.
d	Neck stitches & Shoulder stitches	___ ÷ 3 = ___	100 ÷ 3 = **33** 33 stitches for each shoulder, 34 stitches for neck	Divide the number of stitches in the upper front in thirds to calculate the **number of stitches in the neck and shoulders**. If your number of stitches is not a multiple of 3, include the extra stitches with the neck. Make sure you have the same number of stitches in each shoulder.
e	Sleeve stitches	___ x ___ = ___	20 x 5 = **100**	Multiply the sleeve circumference by your stitch gauge to calculate the **number of sleeve stitches** needed at the top of the sleeve.
f	Cuff stitches	___	**40**	After you knit the body of your sweater, wrap the ribbing around your wrist and count the **number of stitches for the cuff**. For a rough estimate of this number, divide the main number of stitches by 5.

Need a slightly different stitch count? Increase or decrease by a few.

This example has been set up with numbers that clearly demonstrate the simple calculations. Those numbers happen to result in an adult's sweater with a finished chest measurement of 40″ (102 cm) that falls to a generous hip length. If you're not that size, and only a few of us will be, use the guidelines on pages 14 through 16 and measurements you gather for yourself to make a sweater that is customized for its wearer.

| **Knit!** | *option 3: a step-by-step project sheet* | Norway Crewneck Sweater |

For knitters who would like detailed instructions

Use this project sheet if you are not yet comfortable working directly from the sweater-planning diagram. With time, you'll find that you no longer need to refer to these instructions.

Do the calculations on the planning worksheets on pages 127 and 128 so you have the numbers to fill in here.

1 Cast on and knit ribbing

b

With the 29-inch (74-cm) circular needle, cast on ____ stitches (**90% of main number of stitches**). Join, being careful not to twist, place a marker at the beginning of the round, and knit in the round.

Work in k1, p1 ribbing until body measures 2 inches (5 cm), or until ribbing is desired length.

2 Work white section and lice pattern

a

Change to stockinette stitch (knit every round). Increase to ____ stitches (**main number of stitches**) on the first round as follows: *K9, increase 1, repeat from * to end of round.

c

On the next round, knit ____ **back stitches**, place a second marker, knit to end of round. You now have a marker at the beginning of the round and a second marker halfway around, marking the side "seams" of the sweater.

Work even in stockinette stitch, first in white, then changing (when you would

like to) to a black background with white flecks for the lice pattern, until the body measures ____ inches (cm) (**amount of white section plus lice pattern**) from the top of the ribbing. (Or work for the desired length if you are winging it and choosing pattern stitches as you go.)

D

3 Work patterns

You will work the body straight to the shoulder and will machine stitch and cut the fabric at each side "seam" to form the armholes.

Note: Remember to center your stitch patterns or adjust the stitch count as necessary when you begin each new pattern (see pages 33 to 35), and work a full repeat of the pattern stitch of your choice.

Work patterns until the body measures ____ inches (cm) (**total length**) from the cast-on edge.

A

4 Cut armhole openings

At each side seam, measure **armhole depth** (____ inches [cm]) down from the bound-off edge to mark the armhole.

C

With a sewing machine, make 2 rows of stitches on each side of the stitch directly at the side "seam."

At the bottom of this column of stitches, sew back and forth a few times to reinforce the edge.

Cut the armhole open with sharp sewing shears, stopping 1 stitch above the bottom of the machine stitching.

⑤ Cut neckline and join shoulders

(d) Divide the back stitches into thirds. Bind off the ____ **neck stitches** (center third) and put the shoulder stitches on hold.

(d) Divide the front stitches into thirds. Put the ____ **neck stitches** (center third) on a loosely tied piece of scrap yarn and the shoulder stitches on hold. Baste an outline of the neckline with contrasting yarn. The center of the front neckline will probably be about 2 inches (5 cm) below the top row of the fabric and the curve will smoothly run up to the edges of the front-shoulder stitches that are on hold (see page 27). Sew 2 rows of machine stitching next to the basting on the neck-opening side. Cut off the excess neck fabric.

Join the front and back at the shoulders using the three-needle bind-off.

⑥ Cast on and knit cuffs

(f) With double-pointed needles, cast on ____ **cuff stitches.** Place a marker, join, and begin knitting the cuff pattern in the round.

⑦ Begin sleeve increases

When cuffs are 2 inches (5 cm) long or desired length, change to pattern stitches of your choice. Usually sweaters in this style have one or two small pattern bands above the cuff, then a large section of lice pattern, followed by two or three pattern bands at the shoulder.

AT THE SAME TIME, begin increasing for the sleeve as follows: On every 4th round, knit 1, increase 1, work in pattern until 2 stitches before end of round, increase 1, knit 1.

Change to the 16-inch (40-cm) circular needle when the stitches no longer fit comfortably on the double-pointed needles.

Keep an eye on the shape of your sleeve and measure it against your model sweater or try your sleeve on after every few inches (cm) to make sure the sleeve is increasing at a comfortable rate. If your sleeve is becoming wide too quickly, start increasing every 6th round. If it is not widening enough, start increasing every 3rd round.

(e) **(B)** Continue increasing until you have ____ **sleeve stitches** and then work even until the sleeve is ____ inches (cm) long **(sleeve length)**.

⑧ Knit facing and bind off sleeve

Work reverse stockinette stitch (purl every round) for ½ inch (1.25 cm) for armhole facing. Bind off all stitches.

Make second sleeve the same way as the first, steps 6 through 8.

⑨ Armholes and facings

Sew sleeves into armholes. Tack down facings, covering the cut edges of the armholes.

⑩ Neckband

Option 1: See page 159 for a neckband that covers the cut edges.

Option 2: Starting at the left shoulder with the right side facing and using the 16-inch (40 cm) circular needle or double-pointed needles, pick up stitches down the left side of the neck

~~~~~~~~~~~~~~~~~~~~~~~~~~~~~~

Tip: The basic guideline for picking up stitches comes from your gauge. For each inch (cm) of edge, pick up approximately the number of stitches in an inch (cm) of your gauge swatch, fudging on the "slightly less than" side.

front, around the cut curve of the front neckline on the body side of the machine stitching, up the right side of the neck front, and across the bound-off stitches at the back neck.

If you end up with an odd number of stitches, increase one stitch on the first round of the neckband so you have an even number of stitches for working the ribbing.

Work in k1, p1 ribbing for 1 inch (2.5 cm), or the desired height of the neckband.

Bind off loosely in pattern.

Weave in the ends.

The Andes

Although knitting was brought to the Andes by the Spanish, the people of South America already had developed longstanding textile traditions. Using llama and alpaca fiber, the Inca people wove intricate, colorful belts, ponchos, blankets, and bags. When the Spanish came, they brought sheep with them and tried to force the Andean people to raise sheep instead of the llamas and alpacas that were adapted to the local environment.

But the people never gave up on their local animals, and today llama and alpaca yarn is widely available. Llama yarn is strong and well suited to making outerwear garments, sturdy bags, and home décor accessories. Alpaca yarn is incredibly soft and knits up into luxurious and very warm sweaters and caps.

In the mountains of Peru, Bolivia, Chile, Argentina, and Ecuador, the descendants of the Incas use both natural-fiber and synthetic yarns to knit many types of accessories. The women use drop spindles to cre-ate tightly spun yarn that knits up with a tight tension to form a uniquely dense and weatherproof fabric. In recent decades, synthetic yarns have become available in South America at very affordable prices, and women have started using these economi-cal yarns to cut down on manual labor. This doesn't eliminate the spinning process entirely, however, because the women re-spin the commercial yarn to achieve the tight twist they prefer. Still, this is probably less than one-quarter of the work required to spin yarn from scratch.

Synthetic yarns come pre-dyed in many bright, even fluores-cent, colors. But in order to achieve a range of colors, natural-fiber yarns must be dyed by hand. For centuries, the Inca people used natural dyes. More recently, women have been using synthetic dyes to create brighter colors than are possible to achieve with natural dyes. Natural-colored yarns are also popular.

Steeks and Andean-style knitting and puntas: you can make this chapter's sweaters without these techniques, but you'll miss a bunch of the fun!

Although women spin and dye yarn, men and boys do much of the knitting in South America. Men wear tight-fitted caps with ear flaps, known as *chullos*, that they knit for themselves. Boys learn to knit at a young age, and except for the first *chullo* each infant wears as a baby, a boy makes all of his caps himself. Using bicycle spokes or fine wires for knitting needles, they knit at a very fine gauge—sometimes as much as 20 stitches per inch (79 stitches/10 cm)—with multiple colors. The resulting caps are windproof. The *chullos* are knitted in the round except for the ear flaps, which are added after the main portion of the cap has been completed. Today, younger men and boys wear baseball caps over their *chullos*.

Women knit purses in many different sizes and shapes. Most are small, compared to North American pocketbooks, and they

Chapter

6

CHAPTER HIGHLIGHTS

Skills

☑ Two-color patterning in the round

☑ Andean-style knitting

Techniques

☑ Puntas for edge trims (as a base for knitting or sewn on)

☑ Steeks for armholes

Garment styling

☑ Drop shoulder, standard pullover style

☑ Upper body sections worked in the round

☑ Sleeves picked up at shoulder and knitted down to wrist

contain many tiny pockets to store change, small personal items, and amulets. The purses are knitted in the round, with stitches for the pocket openings knitted in scrap yarn that is later removed so stitches can be picked up to add the small pockets. Simple purses may be rectangular or oblong, with only one or two small pockets. Complex purses may be in the shapes of animals or people or in diamond shapes, and they often have many pockets. They may be decorated with tassels and coins for good luck.

Men and women knit other accessories as well, including mittens, gloves, and leg warmers.

The Andean people do not knit sweaters. However, their techniques and color patterns can easily be adapted for use in making sweaters. By using the bright colors and decorative edgings that are traditional in Andean designs, you can create garments that evoke the spirit and style of the ancient Incas. While the background of a Norwegian sweater is black or a dark solid color on the entire garment, the background on Andean knitting usually changes with each pattern. Sometimes the background changes within a pattern. Solid white Inca crosses, for example, may be knitted against a rainbow background that changes color every few rows.

Tips: Don't be intimidated by Andean-style knitting, even though it may seem very different from what you're used to.

The parts of the technique can be used separately while you become familiar with them.

To practice, you may find it easier to start a small tube of stockinette stitch using your regular knitting technique and five double-pointed needles. Arrange your stitches so there is an equal number on each of four needles, and knit with the fifth. (Even if you normally use only four double-pointed needles, use five for working with Andean techniques.) Then switch to the Andean technique and knit a few inches (several cm) to get some practice tensioning the yarn. You will change directions, but this is just a practice piece so that won't be a problem.

You can also work on the far, purl side of the knitting while tensioning the yarn and forming the stitches in any way you like. Then you can pick up speed by neck-tensioning and using the thumb-flick method of forming the stitches.

The only thing you need to know is that once you've started working on the purl side of the fabric you'll need to continue working on the purl side because the direction in which the stitches move has been established. (You can turn around and go in the other direction, but you'll need to figure out a way to disguise the small gap at the turning point.)

Start with the *monedero*. Make it any size. You'll find a use for it and you'll begin making the techniques your own.

Techniques

Knitters in the Andes tension their yarn around their necks and work in the round from the inside of the project. The right side of the work shows on the outside of the knitting, as in standard North American techniques, but the knitter works from the inside, purling the stitches in stockinette stitch.

Tensioning the yarn

To tension the yarn in Andean-style knitting, put the ball of yarn on your left and run the yarn around the back of your neck from left to right. (Wearing a turtleneck or a shirt with a collar will keep you from getting friction burn on the back of your neck!) The yarn should be taut, like a guitar string. If you need extra tension, try putting some extra drag on it by setting your yarn on the floor or running it under your left arm before it goes around your neck.

Position your knitting so the join where the working yarn is attached to the knitting is away from you, on the far side of the tube.

How to tension the yarn around your neck.

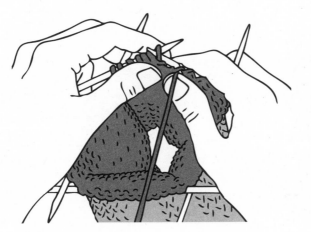

How to hold the knitting: work on the far, purl side of the fabric.

Andean purling

Because Andean knitting is worked from the inside, all stitches are purled in stockinette stitch.

You will be working on the inside of the tube of knitting, looking at the purl side (wrong side). The knit side (right side) will be formed on the outside of the tube.

1. Insert the right needle into the front loop of the first stitch on the left needle as if you were making a regular purl stitch.

2. With the yarn tensioned around your neck, use your left thumb to pull the yarn around the back of the front needle from right to left.

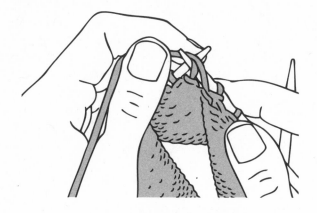

Use your left thumb to pull the yarn—under tension around your neck—around the back of the front needle.

3. Pull out your thumb and let the yarn catch on the needle. If the yarn falls off the needle, your yarn is not tensioned tightly enough.

4. Pull the yarn through.

When you pull your thumb out, the working yarn will catch on the needle and you can pull the new loop through.

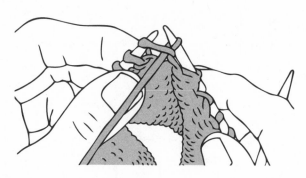

5. Drop the old stitch from the left needle. You now have one new stitch on the right needle.

Working with two colors

When you are working with two colors on the same row, put your right thumb between the two strands of yarn. When you purl with the main color, lift the contrasting color *up* and out of the way. When you purl with the contrasting color, pull the main color *down* and out of the way. This keeps the yarns from twisting together and getting tangled.

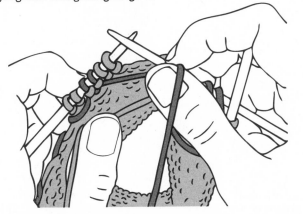

When you work with two colors, separate them with your right thumb. When you switch colors, the left thumb controls the color that is active and the right thumb holds the inactive color out of the way.

Puntas

Puntas are small scallops that are used on the edges of *chullos*. These scallops also make a decorative edging appropriate for a woman's or girl's sweater. You will need both a crochet hook and a knitting needle. The crochet hook should be about the same size as the knitting needle.

Each scallop will use 7 stitches from the crocheted chain base from which it is worked and will leave 4 ready-to-knit stitches on your knitting needle.

1. With a crochet hook, make the foundation for your puntas. You will use a multiple of seven crocheted stitches and your chain will be about 1.75 times the length of your cast-on edge, but just chain a workable length and don't worry about how many stitches or how long a starting chain you have. You can add or remove stitches as you go along. Pull the last loop of the chain so it is very large and the chain won't unravel while you are working. Don't fasten off.

The technique you will use, picking up stitches through the bumps on the backs of the chains, is also used when picking up stitches through a crocheted chain for a provisional cast-on, in case you are familiar with that idea. However, in this case the crocheted chain is not removed later. It becomes part of the final results. When done in a contrasting color, it creates a decorative line along the outside edge of the puntas.

2. Attach a second color to the end of the chain with a slip-knot.

3. Hold one knitting needle in your right hand for steps 3 through 5. First, pick up 4 stitches through the first four bumps on the back of the chain.

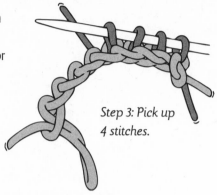

Step 3: Pick up 4 stitches.

4. With the working needle in your left hand, slip the second stitch on the right needle over the first stitch and drop it off the needle, as you do when binding off a stitch. Pick up 1 stitch in the next loop on the crocheted chain.

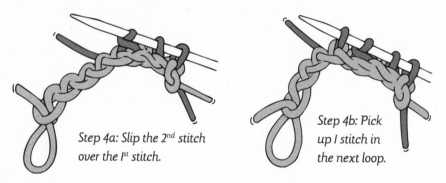

Step 4a: Slip the 2nd stitch over the 1st stitch.

Step 4b: Pick up 1 stitch in the next loop.

5. Slip the 2nd and 3rd stitches on the right needle over the first and drop them both off the needle. Pick up 1 stitch through the back of the chain.

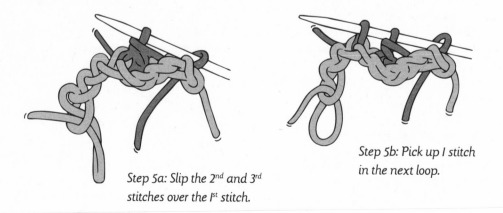

Step 5a: Slip the 2nd and 3rd stitches over the 1st stitch.

Step 5b: Pick up 1 stitch in the next loop.

6. Turn the work, pick up your second knitting needle, and purl 3 stitches.

7. Turn and knit 3 stitches.

8. Slip 1 bump from the chain to the right needle.

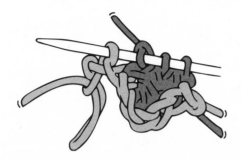

When you complete each punta, you will have 4 new stitches on the needle. The final one will be a crochet-chain loop. If you made the chain in a contrasting color, that color will form the edge of the row of puntas.

Repeat steps 3 through 8 for the desired number of puntas.

If you are working in two colors as described, each punta will leave 4 stitches on the knitting needle, 3 of the second color followed by 1 of the chain color. Your series of puntas will end with a picked-up bump from the chain.

Color patterns, simple to complex. . . .

The color patterns used on Andean caps, bags, and accessories cover a wide range of complexity. There are simple stripes and checkers, complicated geometric designs (such as zigzags and Inca crosses), and pictorial representations of people and animals. Many of the symbols carry sacred meanings and have been in use for centuries in the mountains and plains of the Andes.

The *coca leaf* has been integral to Andean culture for millennia. Today, workers chew the leaves of the coca plant for stamina during a long day's work. It is said that the leaves also provide relief for high-altitude sickness.

Animal motifs are popular on Andean knitting. Guard dogs are used as protective amulets; birds bring good news; and livestock animals are reminders of the still-rural lifestyle in the region.

Cross motifs are used to remember a recently deceased friend or loved one, as well as to provide protection over the fields during the growing season.

Zigzags may symbolize rivers or roads, which provide transportation through the mountainous terrain. They may also represent serpents, who bring wisdom and knowledge of the ancient past to the wearer, or earthworms, who bring fertility to the fields.

Pattern stitches

Waves

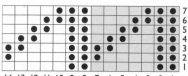

	12	11	10	9	8	7	6	5	4	3	2	1
6	●	●	●	●		●	●	●	●	●	●	●
5				●	●	●			●	●	●	●
4			●	●	●				●	●	●	
3			●	●	●			●	●	●		
2		●	●	●			●	●	●			
1		●	●	●			●	●	●			

Repeat: 6 stitches by 5 or 6 rows

Row 6 is optional, depending on how you sequence your patterns

Zigzags

	14	13	12	11	10	9	8	7	6	5	4	3	2	1
7					●	●	●					●	●	●
6				●	●	●					●	●	●	●
5			●	●	●					●	●		●	●
4		●	●	●			●	●					●	●
3	●	●	●			●	●	●					●	●
2	●	●			●	●	●						●	●
1					●	●	●	●					●	●

Repeat: 7 stitches by 7 rows

Coca leaf

	12	11	10	9	8	7	6	5	4	3	2	1
13												
12		●	●	●					●	●	●	
11		●	●			●	●			●	●	
10		●	●	●		●	●		●	●	●	
9												
8												
7												
6			●	●	●		●	●	●			
5		●	●	●			●	●		●	●	
4	●	●			●	●				●	●	●
3	●	●			●	●			●	●		
2	●	●	●			●	●		●	●	●	
1												

Repeat: 12 stitches by 13 rows

(plus 1 stitch to balance)

You can work all of the rows, or just rows 1 to 7 for a smaller pattern.

Small checks

Repeat: 4 stitches by 4 rows

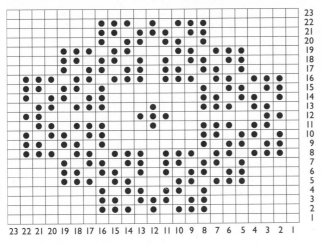

Repeat: 23 stitches by 23 rows

Inca cross

Animal motifs

Here are a llama, a dog, and a cat.

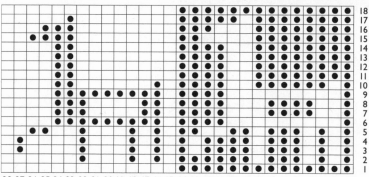

Repeat: 14 or 28 stitches by 18 rows

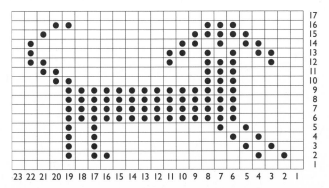

Repeat: 23 stitches by 17 rows

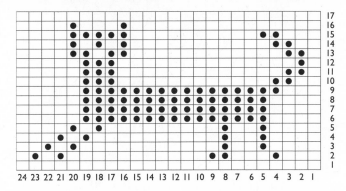

Repeat: 24 stitches by 17 rows

143

Monedero (Change Purse)

This small change purse will give you a chance to practice knitting with two colors in the round, and to use the three-needle bind-off to close the bottom of the bag. The bag can be made in any size and using any pattern stitches. The eyelets-and-drawstring closure is made using the same techniques as the neck embellishment on a Dutch fisher-man's sweater (as on pages 59 and 67, step 10).

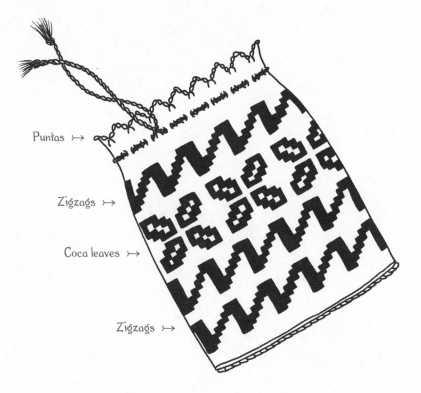

Puntas ⟶

Zigzags ⟶

Coca leaves ⟶

Zigzags ⟶

- ✓ Color patterning
- ✓ Worked in the round, Andean-style
- ✓ Knitted top to bottom, puntas to three-needle bind-off
- ✓ Easy eyelets for drawstring

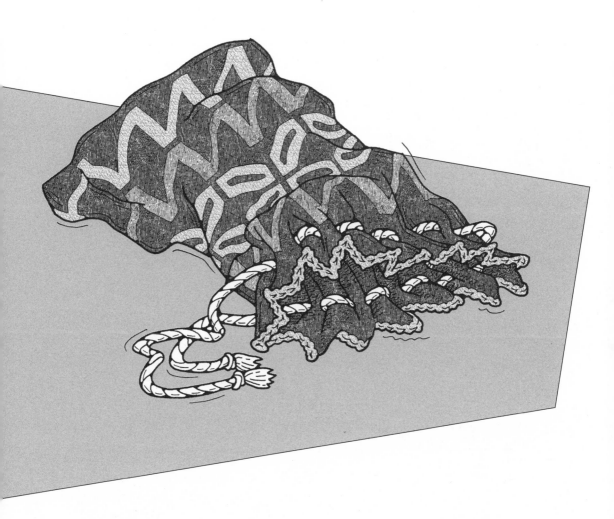

For these bags, you can just start with a stitch count that is a multiple of your patterns and wing

it. You'll get something useful. At 6 stitches and 7½ rows to the inch (24 stitches and 30 rows

to 10 cm), the pattern sequence shown on these two pages produces a bag that's 9½ inches (24 cm)

in circumference (4¾ inches [12 cm] across) and about 6½ inches (16.5 cm) long, not including the

puntas.

Get ready   *yarn & needles*

Yarn

Smooth yarn will show off stitches and color patterns best. Llama yarn will make a sturdy, durable bag. Alpaca will make a softer, more luxurious purse. This is a good project on which to try out different colors and fibers. Make four or five little bags to experiment, and you'll be way ahead on your holiday gift shopping.

Any weight of yarn will work, but for practice I suggest a medium-weight yarn and U.S. size 7 or 8 (4.5 or 5 mm) knitting needles. Approximately 200 yards (182 m) of medium-weight yarn—total of all colors—will make a medium-sized bag.

Needle guidelines are on page 22.

Knitting needles and crochet hook

In a size appropriate for the yarn you've chosen:

✧ If your bag will be less than 12 inches (30.5 cm) in circumference, you will need a set of 5 double-pointed needles to work in the Andean technique

✧ If your bag will be more than 12 inches (30.5 cm) in circumference, you can use a short circular needle

✧ Crochet hook in a size close to the size of the knitting needles, for making puntas (optional)

Get set   *stitches, gauge & size*

Stitches and gauge

① Select the stitch for your bag. Use the pattern shown on the sample illustration, or choose your favorite from the Andean color charts.

② I wouldn't bother making a gauge swatch for this bag, although you can use the bag itself as a swatch for a sweater if you will be using the same yarn and needles. If you want to make the bag a specific size, you will need to make a gauge swatch.

Even though gauge is not important for a bag, it is a good idea to practice each pattern stitch to make sure you enjoy knitting the stitch and to learn the pattern.

③ If you made a gauge swatch, measure the stitch gauge and write it on the planning worksheet on page 148.

Size

① Determine how wide and long you want your bag to be, and write the measurements in the boxes on the planning worksheet on page 148.

② Use the calculations on the work-sheet to figure the remaining numbers.

③ Transfer the numbers to the visual plan below or the step-by-step instructions on page 149, depending on how much guiding detail you would like to have while you knit.

Knit! *option I: using a visual plan*

The Andes
Monedero

For knitters who are ready to work from the basic concept

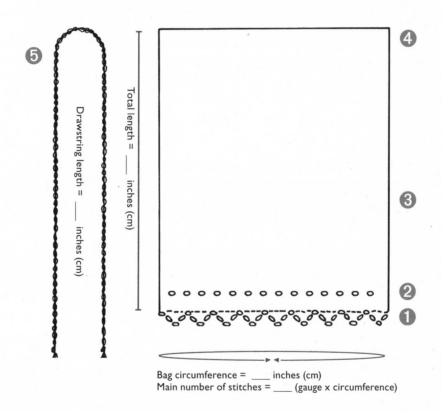

⑤

Drawstring length = ____ inches (cm)

Total length = ____ inches (cm)

④

③

②

①

Bag circumference = ____ inches (cm)
Main number of stitches = ____ (gauge x circumference)

① Cast on ____ stitches OR make puntas

② Work eyelets for drawstring

③ Work patterns for desired length

④ Close bottom with three-needle bind-off

⑤ Make drawstring and thread through eyelets

Knit! *option 2: using a planning worksheet*   The Andes
Monedero

For knitters who want to plan thoroughly in advance

Measurements and stitch counts

	Calculation	Example	Description
Stitch gauge	____ stitches = 1 inch or 1 cm	**5** stitches = 1 inch	**Gauge** is not critical for a bag.
Width	____ inches (cm)	**5** inches	Desired **width** of bag.
Length	____ inches (cm)	**6** inches	Desired **length** of bag.
Circumference	____ x 2 = ____	5 x 2 = **10** inches	Double the width to calculate the **circumference** of the bag.
Main number of stitches	____ x ____ = ____	10 x 5 = **50** stitches	Multiply the circumference by your stitch gauge to calculate the **main number of stitches**. Working the puntas around the top edge will give you a number of stitches that is a multiple of 4. Increase or decrease after working the puntas to achieve a main number that will accommodate the repeat of your first pattern.

Need a slightly different stitch count? Increase or decrease by a few.

| **Knit!** | *option 3: a step-by-step project sheet* | The Andes Monedero |

For knitters who would like detailed instructions

Do the calculations on the planning worksheet on page 148 so you have the numbers to fill in here.

The instructions for this bag are written for Andean-style knitting, described on pages 136 and 137. You can, of course, use another color-knitting technique if you prefer.

❶ Cast on

You can make this bag with a plain edge or with puntas.

For a plain edge, cast on _____ stitches (**main number of stitches**). Arrange the stitches evenly on 4 double-pointed needles. Join, being careful not to twist, to knit in the round.

If you have never knitted using the Andean technique before, knit 1 round plain, then begin using the Andean technique.

For an edge with puntas, make a crochet chain a few inches (cm) longer than the desired circumference of your bag. Remember that you can add or remove chains as needed. Make enough puntas (described on pages 137 to 139) to equal the desired circumference. Each completed punta will leave four ready-to-knit stitches on your needle. Arrange the stitches evenly on 4 double-pointed needles or a short circular needle, as appropriate for your bag. Join, being careful not to twist, to knit in the round.

❷ Work eyelets for drawstring

Work 3 rounds.

Work eyelets as follows: Purl 1, (yarn over, p2tog) around. If you have an extra stitch at the end of the round, purl it.

Work 3 rounds.

❸ Work bag body

Begin working your selected pattern stitches (examples are on pages 140 to 143).

Remember to center your stitch patterns or adjust the stitch count as necessary when you begin each new pattern (see pages 33 to 35). Because you are working the bag from the top down, you may want to work the charts from the top down as well, especially if you use the animals.

❹ Finish

Put the first half of the stitches on one needle and the second half on a second needle. With a third needle, join the two pieces together using the three-needle bind-off (see page 35).

Weave in the ends.

❺ Drawstring

Make a drawstring following the instructions on page 67. Thread it through the eyelets, and tie the ends of the drawstring together with an overhand knot.

Unisex Pullover

Make this sweater in neutral shades for a classic look that even the most conservative man or boy will wear. Alpaca yarn comes in almost thirty different natural colors, making it an excellent choice for this design. Start with black and off-white, and add three or four shades of reds and browns to complete your palette.

For a flamboyant, Andean flair, work the design in bright, neon colors. If you make this choice, the selection of yarn and fiber can be as wild as your imagination.

The sample shows alternating bands of light-on-dark and dark-on-light patterning

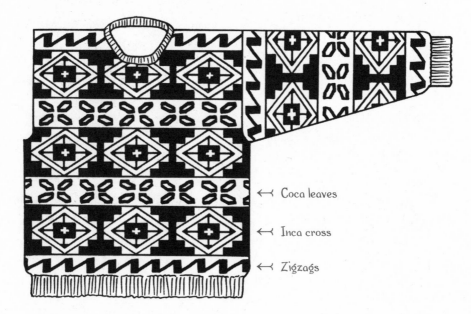

←⟨ Coca leaves

←⟨ Inca cross

←⟨ Zigzags

✓ Color patterning: in horizontal bands

✓ Worked in the round throughout, in Andean-style, with steeked armholes

✓ Steeked neckline finished with picked-up ribbing

✓ Sleeves picked up around armholes and worked down to ribbed cuffs

The illustrations here and opposite show a sweater with a 40-inch (101.6-cm) body circumference

and 24-inch (61-cm) body length (including 2 inches [5 cm] of ribbing) in chunky-weight yarn with

3½ stitches and 5 rows to the inch (14 stitches and 20 rows to 10 cm).

Get ready *yarn & needles*

Yarn

As with the *monedero* (change purse), a smooth yarn will show off the colors and stitches best. But on this garment a yarn with a subtle texture will also yield interesting results. Even a slightly fuzzy yarn would be fun. However, novelty yarns, like eyelash or highly textured fibers, will make the patterns difficult to see.

Any weight of yarn will work, but for practice I suggest a medium-weight yarn and U.S. size 7 or 8 (4.5 or 5 mm) knitting needles.

Needle guidelines are on page 22. See the yarn estimate table on page 23 for yardages.

Knitting needles

In a size appropriate for the yarn you've chosen:

✧ Circular needle for body: for most adult sweaters, you will want a needle at least 29 inches (74 cm) long

✧ Circular needle for upper sleeves and neckband: 16 inches (40 cm) long

✧ Double-pointed needles for lower sleeves: set of 4 or 5

Optional for ribbings: Two sizes smaller than primary needles::

✧ Circular needle for body ribbing: for most adult sweaters, you will want a needle at least 29 inches (74 cm) long

✧ Double-pointed needles for cuffs: set of 4 or 5

If you decide to use smaller needles for the ribbings, I'll count on you to know when to switch between needle sizes. Everyone else: Work on same-size needles with me. You'll do fine.

| **Get set** *stitches, gauge & size* | The Andes
Unisex Pullover |

Stitches and gauge

① Select pattern stitches for your sweater. Use the combination shown in the illustrations on pages 150 and 151 or choose your own combination of stitches. You can choose your pattern stitches before you begin, or make up the design as you go.

② Make a gauge swatch in stockinette stitch.

③ Measure your gauge. Write the stitch gauge and row gauge on the sweater-planning worksheet on page 155.

Size

① Measure your favorite sweater or use the size charts on page 16 to determine the basic dimensions for your sweater. Write the measurements on the visual plan on page 154 and the sweater-planning worksheet on page 155.

② Use the calculations on the worksheets on pages 155 and 156 to figure the remaining numbers before you start, or just calculate each new number as you need it.

③ Transfer the resulting numbers to the visual plan on page 154 or the step-by-step instructions on pages 157 to 159, depending on how much guiding detail you would like to have while you knit.

> The color patterns inspired by Andean textiles are on pages 140 to 143.

Knit! *option I: using a visual plan*

The Andes
Unisex Pullover

For knitters who are ready to work from the basic concept

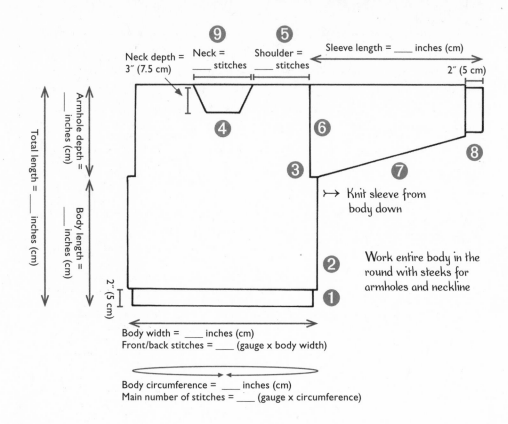

Neck depth = 3″ (7.5 cm)

Neck = ____ stitches

Shoulder = ____ stitches

Sleeve length = ____ inches (cm)

2″ (5 cm)

Armhole depth = ____ inches (cm)

Total length = ____ inches (cm)

Body length = ____ inches (cm)

2″ (5 cm)

Knit sleeve from body down

Work entire body in the round with steeks for armholes and neckline

Body width = ____ inches (cm)
Front/back stitches = ____ (gauge x body width)

Body circumference = ____ inches (cm)
Main number of stitches = ____ (gauge x circumference)

BODY

❶ Cast on ____ stitches (90% of main number of stitches) and knit ribbing

❷ Increase to ____ stitches (main number of stitches) and work patterns

❸ Work armhole steeks

❹ Work neckline steek; decrease until ____ stitches remain at each shoulder

❺ Open steeks and join shoulders: ____ stitches

SLEEVES

❻ Pick up ____ sleeve stitches at armhole

❼ Decrease to ____ cuff stitches

❽ Work ribbing and bind off

FINISH

❾ Work neckband

Knit!	*option 2: using planning worksheets*	The Andes Unisex Pullover

For knitters who want to plan thoroughly in advance

Measurements

	Calculation	**Example**	**Description**
Stitch gauge	____ stitches = 1 inch or 1 cm	**5** stitches = 1 inch	Stitch **gauge** is critical for knitting a sweater that fits properly.
Row gauge	____ rows = 1 inch or 1 cm	**6** rows = 1 inch	**Row gauge** is not critical for this sweater.
Body width	____ inches (cm)	**20** inches	Measure the **width** of the sweater body.
Body circumference	____ x 2 = ____	20 x 2 = **40** inches	Double the body width for the **circumference of the sweater**.
A *Total length*	____ inches (cm)	**24** inches	Measure the **length** of the sweater body.
B *Sleeve length*	____ inches (cm)	**18** inches	Measure the **sleeve length** from wrist to underarm.
Armhole depth	____ ÷ 4 = ____	40 ÷ 4 = **10** inches	Divide the body circumference by 4 to calculate the **armhole depth**.
C *Body length*	____ – ____ = ____	24 – 10 = **14** inches	Subtract the armhole depth from the total body length to calculate the **length of the body from the cast-on edge to the armhole**.
Sleeve circumference	____ x 2 = ____	10 x 2 = **20** inches	Double the armhole depth for the **circumference of the sleeve**.

This example has been set up with numbers that clearly demonstrate the simple calculations. Those numbers happen to result in an adult's sweater with a finished chest measurement of 40″ (102 cm) that falls to a generous hip length. If you're not that size, and only a few of us will be, use the guidelines on pages 14 through 16 and measurements you gather for yourself to make a sweater that is customized for its wearer.

Stitch counts

		Calculation	Example	Description
a	Main number of stitches	___ x ___ = ___	40 x 5 = **200**	Multiply the body circumference by your stitch gauge to calculate the **main number of stitches**.
b	90% of main number of stitches	___ x 0.9 = ___	200 x 0.9 = **180**	Take 90 percent of the main number of stitches to calculate the **number of stitches to cast on**. If this is an odd number, add 1 so you have an even number of stitches for working the k1, p1 ribbing.
c	Front stitches & Back stitches	___ ÷ 2 = ___	200 ÷ 2 = **100**	Divide the main number of stitches in half to determine the **number of stitches in the upper front and upper back**.
d	Armhole bind-off stitches	___ stitches (same as stitch-gauge measurement)	**5 stitches**	The **number of stitches to bind off in preparation for the armhole steek** on either side of each side marker is equal to the gauge measurement for 1 inch (2.5 cm) or the nearest whole number.
e	Neck stitches & Shoulder stitches	___ ÷ 3 = ___	100 ÷ 3 = **33** **33** stitches for each shoulder, **34** stitches for neckline	Divide the number of stitches in the upper front in thirds to calculate the **number of stitches in the neck and shoulders**. If your number of stitches is not a multiple of 3, include the extra stitches with the neck. Make sure you have the same number of stitches in each shoulder.
f	Front neck bind-off stitches	___ – 10 = ___	34 – 10 = **24**	Subtract 10 from the total number of neck stitches to calculate the **number of stitches to bind off in preparation for the neck steek**.
g	Adjusted shoulder stitches	___ – ___ = ___	33 – 5 = **28**	Subtract armhole bind-off stitches from shoulder stitches to calculate the **number of stitches at the top of each shoulder**.
h	Sleeve stitches	___ x ___ = ___	20 x 5 = **100**	Multiply the sleeve circumference by your stitch gauge to calculate the **number of sleeve stitches** to pick up at the armhole.
i	Cuff stitches	___	**40**	After you knit the body of your sweater, wrap the ribbing around your wrist and count the **number of stitches for the cuff**. For a rough estimate of this number, divide the body circumference by 5.

Need a slightly different stitch count? Increase or decrease by a few.

Knit! *option 3: a step-by-step project sheet*
The Andes
Unisex Pullover

For knitters who would like detailed instructions

Use this project sheet if you are not yet comfortable working directly from the sweater-planning diagram. With time, you'll find that you no longer need to refer to these instructions.

Do the calculations on the planning worksheets on pages 155 and 156 so you have the numbers to fill in here.

These instructions are written for Andean-style knitting, described on pages 135 and 136.

❶ Cast on and knit ribbing

b

With the 29-inch (74-cm) circular needle, cast on ____ stitches (**90% of main number of stitches**). Join, being careful not to twist, place a marker at the beginning of the round, and knit in the round using the Andean style of holding the work.

(Wait to use the Andean style of tensioning the yarn until you begin the stockinette section in step 2, when it becomes more efficient to use that technique.)

Work in k1, p1 ribbing until body measures 2 inches (5 cm), or until ribbing is desired length.

❷ Work pattern stitches

a

Change to stockinette stitch (purl every round in the Andean technique; see pages 135 and 136). Increase to ____ stitches (**main number of stitches**) on the first round as follows: *P9, increase 1, repeat from * to end of round.

c
c

On the next round, purl ____ **back stitches**, place a second marker, purl to end of round across ____ **front stitches**. You now have a marker at the beginning of the round and a second marker half-way around, marking the side "seams" of the sweater.

Work even in stockinette stitch.

Note: Remember to center your stitch patterns or adjust the stitch count as necessary when you begin each new pattern (see pages 33 to 35), and work a full repeat of the pattern stitch of your choice.

C

Work patterns until the body measures ____ inches (cm) (**body length**) from the cast-on edge.

❸ Work armhole steeks

d

Bind off ____ **armhole bind-off stitches** before and after each side marker. Work around to the first set of bound-off stitches. Place a marker, cast on 7 stitches, place a marker. Do the same at the second set of bound-off stitches. The stitches between these new markers are the armhole steek stitches. Work them in alternating colors on every round (see pages 28 and 29).

A

Work even until the sweater measures 3 inches (7.5 cm) less than **total length** (____ inches [cm]) or ____ inches (cm) long.

157

④ Work neck steek

f

On the front, bind off the center ____ **front neck bind-off stitches**. Work around to the bound-off stitches. Place a marker, cast on 7 stitches, place a marker. The stitches between the markers are the neckline steek stitches. Work them in alternating colors on every round (see pages 28 and 29).

On the next round, decrease 1 stitch before the first neckline steek marker and 1 stitch after the second neckline steek marker to shape the neck opening.

g

Decrease in this manner on every other round until there are ____ **adjusted shoulder stitches** remaining for each shoulder on the front. Work even until

A

the body measures ____ inches (cm) (**total length**) from the cast-on edge.

On the next round, bind off the steek stitches at both armholes, the steek stitches at the front neck, and on the

e

back the center ____ **neck stitches**.

g

You will have four sets of ____ **adjusted shoulder stitches** left. Put them on holders.

⑤ Open steeks and join shoulders

Cut the neck and armhole steeks open with sharp sewing shears. (See pages 28 to 29. If desired, first sew 2 rows of

machine stitching on each side of the stitch you will be cutting.)

Join the front and back at the shoulders using the three-needle bind-off.

⑥ Pick up stitches for sleeves

Beginning at the underarm and using the 16-inch (40-cm) circular needle, pick up ____ **sleeve stitches** around one of the armhole openings. Place a marker, join, and begin working stockinette stitch in the round.

h

Work stockinette stitch in the pattern stitches of your choice.

⑦ Begin sleeve decreases

AT THE SAME TIME, begin decreasing for the sleeve on the 4th round after picking up stitches as follows: On every 4th round, purl 1, p2tog, purl to 3 stitches before the marker, p2tog, purl 1. (The decreases are purls because we're using the Andean technique. They would otherwise be knitted.)

Change to double-pointed needles when the stitches no longer fit comfortably on the circular needle.

Keep an eye on the shape of your sleeve and measure it against your model sweater or try your sleeve on after every few inches (cm) to make sure the sleeve

---

Tip: If you have markers in two colors, use one color for both armhole steeks and a different color for the neckline steek. Then you will be able to tell easily where to make the neckline decreases.

Tip: The basic guideline for picking up stitches comes from your gauge. For each inch (cm) of edge, pick up approximately the number of stitches in an inch (cm) of your gauge swatch, fudging on the "slightly less than" side.

is decreasing at a comfortable rate. If your sleeve is becoming narrow too quickly, start decreasing every 6th round. If it is not narrowing quickly enough, start decreasing every 3rd round.

i Continue decreasing until you have ____ **cuff stitches** and then work even.

B When your sleeve measures 2 inches (5 cm) less than **sleeve length** (____ inches [cm]) or ____ inches (cm), try on the sweater to test the sleeve length. The bottom of the sleeve should fall just above your wrist bone, to leave enough space to knit the cuffs.

If your sleeve reaches **sleeve length** before you have decreased to the number of **cuff stitches**, spread the remaining number of decreases evenly across the next round.

8 Work cuff and bind off sleeve

Change to k1, p1 ribbing. Work in ribbing for 2 inches (5 cm).

Bind off loosely in pattern.

Make second sleeve the same way as the first, steps 6 through 8.

9 Finishing

Neckband

Starting at the left shoulder with the right side facing and using the 16-inch (40-cm) circular needle, pick up stitches down the left side of the neck front, across the front stitches, up the right side of the neck front, and across the back stitches.

If you end up with an odd number of stitches, increase one stitch on the first round of the neckband so you have an even number of stitches for working the ribbing.

Work in k1, p1 ribbing for 1 inch (2.5 cm), or the desired height of the neckband. Purl 1 round (turning ridge). Work in k1, p1 ribbing for 1 inch (2.5 cm).

Bind off loosely in pattern. Fold the neckband to the inside and sew the bound-off edge to the inside at the point where you picked up stitches, making a double-thickness ribbing that encloses the cut neck opening.

On the inside of the body, tack down the cut edges of the armhole steeks.

Weave in the ends.

Girls Only Pullover
(with Boys' Alternative)

This sweater, decorated with a frilly punta trim and knit-
ted cat and dog motifs, is my feminine interpretation of
Andean folk knitting. Whether the recipient is young, or
simply young at heart, this design will delight her.

For a boy, you can make a similar design in neutral colors
without the decorative puntas.

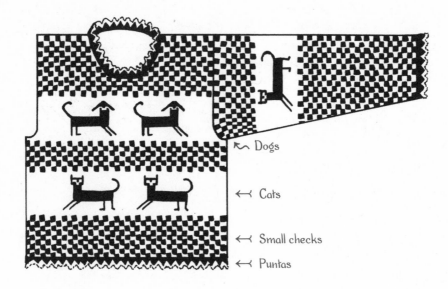

↖ Dogs

← Cats

← Small checks

← Puntas

☑ Color patterning: in horizontal bands

☑ Puntas at all opening edges, including initial cast-on

☑ Worked in the round throughout, Andean-style, with steeked armholes

☑ Steeked neckline, finished with sewn-on puntas

☑ Sleeves picked up around armholes and worked down to wrists, finished with
    sewn-on puntas

This illustration shows a sweater with a 30-inch (76-cm) body circumference and 16-inch (40.6-cm) body length in worsted-weight yarn with 5 stitches and 6 rows to the inch (20 stitches and 24 rows to 10 cm). Do a quick pattern-height calculation (like the one for the Norwegian sweater on pages 115/117 or 125/127) to be sure your animal bands end at least 1 inch (2.5 cm) below the neckline.

Get ready   *how to design your sweater*

Yarn

Wool yarn will knit up into a warm, cozy sweater. You may want to select a machine-washable wool, a blend, or an acrylic yarn to make a washable sweater for a child.

Any weight of yarn will work. The drawings represent garments made with a medium-weight yarn and U.S. size 7 or 8 (4.5 or 5 mm) knitting needles. Because you are using two colors throughout, the knitting will be significantly heavier than when you work with a single color. You may want to consider a slightly lighter yarn, such as DK yarn and U.S. size 5, 6, or 7 (3.75 to 4.5 mm) knitting needles or sportweight yarn and U.S. size 3, 4, or 5 (3.25 to 3.75 mm) knitting needles.

Needle guidelines are on page 22. See the yarn estimate table on page 23 for yardages.

Knitting needles and crochet hook

In a size appropriate for the yarn you've chosen:

✧ Circular needle for body: because this is a child's sweater, you will want a needle 20 to 24 inches (50 to 60 cm) long

✧ Circular needle for puntas and sleeves: 11 to 16 inches (30 to 40 cm) long

✧ Double-pointed needles for lower sleeves: set of 4 or 5

✧ Crochet hook in size close to knitting needles for puntas

| **Get set** *stitches, gauge & size* | The Andes
Girls Only Pullover |

Stitches and gauge

① Select pattern stitches for your sweater. Use the combination shown in the illustrations on pages 160 and 161 or choose your own combination of stitches. You can choose your pattern stitches before you begin, or make up the design as you go.

② Make a gauge swatch in each of the pattern stitches you have chosen.

③ Measure your gauge. Write the stitch gauge and row gauge on the sweater-planning worksheet on page 165.

> The color patterns inspired by Andean textiles are on pages 140 to 143.

Size

① Measure your recipient's favorite sweater or use the size charts on page 16 to determine the basic dimensions for your sweater. Write the measurements on the visual plan on page 164 and the the sweater-planning worksheet on page 165.

② Use the calculations on the worksheets on pages 165 and 166 to figure all the remaining numbers before you start, or just calculate each new number as you need it.

③ Transfer the resulting numbers to the visual plan on page 164 or the step-by-step instructions on pages 167 to 169, depending on how much guiding detail you would like to have while you knit.

Cover sweater story: Andean design

by Debbie O'Neill

I took much the same approach as I did for the Norwegian sweater (page 121). In this case I wanted to use three large motifs—the cats, the dogs, and the flower. Naturally, each motif has a slightly different repeat. I added or subtracted main-color stitches between the pictures to make the repeats work together. After I set up these three larger motifs, I happened to pick smaller motifs that worked with the same stitch count.

I was inspired by traditional Andean knitting, which is very colorful. I chose vibrant yarns and changed the background colors behind the motifs.

The motifs on the body wouldn't work well on the sleeves at the size and gauge I was using—they were quite small. So I worked the sleeves in stripes, using all my colors.

I knitted in the round and steeked the armholes and neck. I used puntas to finish the bottoms of the sleeves and body; they really add flair. I borrowed the boat neck from the Norwegian chapter and finished it with single crochet.

Knit! *option I: using a visual plan*

The Andes
Girls Only Pullover

For knitters who are ready to work from the basic concept

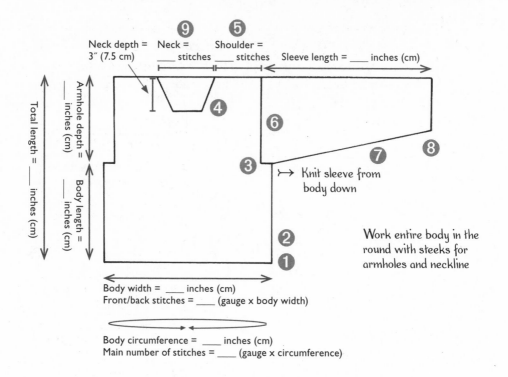

Neck depth = 3″ (7.5 cm)

⑨ Neck = ____ stitches

⑤ Shoulder = ____ stitches

Sleeve length = ____ inches (cm)

Armhole depth = ____ inches (cm)

Total length = ____ inches (cm)

Body length = ____ inches (cm)

④

⑥

③ ⟼ Knit sleeve from body down

⑦ ⑧

②

①

Work entire body in the round with steeks for armholes and neckline

Body width = ____ inches (cm)
Front/back stitches = ____ (gauge x body width)

Body circumference = ____ inches (cm)
Main number of stitches = ____ (gauge x circumference)

PUNTAS

① Work punta edging to produce ____ stitches (**main number of stitches**)

BODY

② Work pattern stitches

③ Work armhole steeks (____ stitches)

④ Work neckline steek; decrease until ____ stitches remain at each shoulder

⑤ Open steeks and join shoulders: ____ stitches

SLEEVES

⑥ Pick up ____ sleeve stitches at armhole

⑦ Decrease to ____ cuff stitches

⑧ Work puntas and sew to lower edges of sleeves

FINISH

⑨ Work neckband or punta neck trim

Knit! *option 2: using planning worksheets*

The Andes
Girls Only Pullover

For knitters who want to plan thoroughly in advance

Measurements

	Calculation	Example	Description
Stitch gauge	____ stitches = 1 inch or 1 cm	**5** stitches = 1 inch	**Stitch gauge** is critical for knitting a sweater that fits properly.
Row gauge	____ stitches = 1 inch or 1 cm	**6** rows = 1 inch	**Row gauge** is not critical for this sweater.
Body width	____ inches (cm)	**15** inches	Measure the **width** of the desired sweater body.
Body circumference	____ x 2 = ____	15 x 2 = **30** inches	Double the body width for the **circumference of the sweater**.
Total length	____ inches (cm)	**16** inches	Measure the **length** of the desired sweater body.
Sleeve length	____ inches (cm)	**15** inches	Measure the **sleeve length** from wrist to underarm.
Armhole depth	____ ÷ 4 = ____	30 ÷ 4 = **7½** inches	Divide the body circumference by 4 to calculate the **armhole depth**.
Body length	____ – ____ = ____	16 – 7½ = **8½** inches	Subtract the armhole depth from the total body length to calculate the **length of the body from the cast-on edge to the armhole**.
Sleeve circumference	____ x 2 = ____	7½ x 2 = **15** inches	Double the armhole depth for the **circumference of the upper sleeve**.

This example has been set up with numbers that clearly demonstrate the simple calculations. Those numbers happen to result in an child's sweater with a finished chest measurement of 26½″ (67 cm) that extends just below the waistline—approximately a size 8. If you need a different size, use the guidelines on pages 14 through 16 and measurements you gather for yourself to make a sweater that is customized for its wearer.

Stitch counts

	Calculation	Example	Description
a Main number of stitches	___ x ___ = ___	30 x 5 = **150** **152** (multiple of 4)	Multiply the body circumference by your stitch gauge to calculate the **main number of stitches**. Because each punta ends up with 4 stitches, round up or down so that your main number is a multiple of 4.
b Front stitches & Back stitches	___ ÷ 2 = ___	152 ÷ 2 = **76**	Divide the main number of stitches in half to determine the **number of stitches in the front and back**.
c Armhole bind-off stitches	___ stitches (same as stitch gauge)	5 stitches	The **number of stitches to bind off in preparation for the armhole steek** on either side of each side marker is equal to the gauge measurement for 1 inch (2.5 cm) or the nearest whole number. (For a tiny child, you may want to cast off half as many stitches at each armhole.)
d Neck stitches & Shoulder stitches	___ ÷ 3 = ___	76 ÷ 3 = **25** **25** stitches for each shoulder, **26** stitches for neck	Divide the number of stitches in the upper front in thirds to calculate the **number of stitches in the neck and shoulders**. If your number of stitches is not a multiple of 3, include the extra stitches with the neck. Make sure you have the same number of stitches in each shoulder.
e Front neck bind-off stitches	___ − 8 = ___	26 − 8 = **18**	Subtract 8 from the total number of neck stitches to calculate the **number of stitches to bind off in preparation for the neck steek**.
f Adjusted shoulder stitches	___ − ___ = ___	25 − 5 = **20**	Subtract armhole bind-off stitches from shoulder stitches to calculate the **number of stitches at the top of each shoulder**.
g Sleeve stitches	___ x ___ = ___	15 x 5 = **75**	Multiply the sleeve circumference by your stitch gauge to calculate the **number of sleeve stitches** needed to pick up at the armhole.
h Cuff stitches	___	36	After you knit the body of your sweater, wrap the ribbing around your wrist and count the **number of stitches for the cuff**. Aim for a multiple of 4 so the punta trim will come out even. For a rough estimate of this number, divide the body circumference by 5.

Need a slightly different stitch count? Increase or decrease by a few.

Knit! *option 3: a step-by-step project sheet*	The Andes
	Girls Only Pullover

For knitters who would like detailed instructions

Use this project sheet if you are not yet comfortable working directly from the sweater-planning diagram. With time, you'll find that you no longer need to refer to these instructions.

Do the calculations on the planning worksheets so you have the numbers to fill in here.

These instructions are written for Andean-style knitting, described on pages 135 and 136.

❶ Punta trim

Make a crochet chain a few inches (cm) longer than the desired circumference of your sweater. Remember that you can add or remove chains as needed. Work the puntas onto the circular needle that you will use for the body of the sweater.

Make enough puntas (pages 137 to 139) to equal the desired circumference or ____ stitches (**main number of stitches**). Each completed punta will leave four ready-to-knit stitches on your needle.

Join to knit in the round, being careful not to twist the stitches. Place a marker at the beginning of the round. Set up your work for the Andean style of tensioning the yarn and holding the fabric.

❷ Work pattern stitches

Begin working stockinette stitch (purl every round in the Andean technique).

Purl ____ **back stitches**, place a second marker, purl to end of round across ____ **front stitches**. You now have a marker at the beginning of the round and a second marker halfway around, marking the side "seams" of the sweater.

Work even in stockinette stitch in the patterns and colors of your choice.

Note: Remember to center your stitch patterns or adjust the stitch count as necessary when you begin each new pattern (see pages 33 to 35), and work a full repeat of the pattern stitch of your choice.

Work patterns until the body measures ____ inches (cm) (**body length**) from the puntas.

❸ Work armhole steeks

Bind off ____ **armhole bind-off stitches** before and after each side marker. Work around to the first set of bound-off stitches. Place a marker, cast on 7 stitches, place a marker. Do the same at the second set of bound-off stitches. The stitches between these new markers are the armhole steek stitches. Work them in alternating colors on every round (see pages 28 and 29).

Work even until the sweater measures 3 inches (7.5 cm) less than **total length** (____ inches [cm] from the puntas) or ____ inches (cm).

Work neck steek

 On the front, bind off the center ____ **front neck bind-off stitches**. Work around to the bound-off stitches. Place a marker, cast on 7 stitches, place a marker. The stitches between the markers are the neckline steek stitches. Work them in alternating colors on every round (see pages 28 and 29).

On the next round, decrease 1 stitch before the first neckline steek marker and 1 stitch after the second neckline steek marker to shape the neck opening.

 Decrease in this manner on every other round until there are ____ **adjusted shoulder stitches** remaining for each shoulder on the front. Work even until the body measures ____ inches (cm) (**total length**) from the puntas.

On the next round, bind off the steek stitches at both armholes, the steek stitches at the front neck, and on the back the center ____ **neck stitches**.

 You will have four sets of ____ **adjusted shoulder stitches** left. Put them on holders.

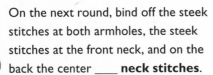 **Open steeks and join shoulders**

Cut the neck and armhole steeks open with sharp sewing shears. (See pages 28 to 29. If desired, first sew 2 rows of machine stitching on each side of the stitch you will be cutting.)

Join the front and back at the shoulders using the three-needle bind-off. Have right sides facing while you work the bind-off if you want the shoulder seams to be relatively invisible and have the wrong sides facing if you want the shoulder seam to be a decorative element on the outside.

⑥ Pick up stitches for sleeves

Beginning at the underarm and using the 16-inch (40-cm) circular needle or, for smaller sizes, double-pointed needles, pick up ____ **sleeve stitches** around one of the armhole openings. Place a marker, join, and begin working stockinette stitch in the round.

Work stockinette stitch in the pattern stitches of your choice.

⑦ Begin sleeve decreases

AT THE SAME TIME, begin decreasing for the sleeve on the 4th round after picking up stitches as follows: On every 4th round, purl 1, p2tog, purl to 3 stitches before the marker, p2tog, purl 1. (The decreases are purls because we're using the Andean technique. They would otherwise be knitted.)

Tip: If you have markers in two colors, use one color for both armhole steeks and a different color for the neckline steek. Then you will be able to tell easily where to make the neckline decreases.

Tip: The basic guideline for picking up stitches comes from your gauge. For each inch (cm) of edge, pick up approximately the number of stitches in an inch (cm) of your gauge swatch, fudging on the "slightly less than" side.

If you are using a circular needle, change to the double-pointed needles when the stitches no longer fit comfortably on it.

Keep an eye on the shape of your sleeve and measure it against your model sweater or try your sleeve on after every few inches (cm) to make sure the sleeve is decreasing at a comfortable rate. If your sleeve is becoming narrow too quickly, start decreasing every 6th round. If it is not narrowing quickly enough, start decreasing every 3rd round.

Continue decreasing until you have ____ **cuff stitches** and then work even until sleeve is ____ inches (cm) long (**sleeve length**).

If your sleeve reaches **sleeve length** before you have decreased to the number of **cuff stitches**, spread the remaining number of decreases evenly across the next round.

8 Bind off and add punta trim

Bind off loosely in pattern.

Make puntas and sew them onto the cuffs.

Make second sleeve the same way as the first, steps 6 through 8.

9 Finishing

Neckband

Make a neckband as described for the Unisex Pullover on page 159, or make a string of puntas and sew them onto the neckline.

On the inside of the body, tack down the cut edges of any steeks that have not been otherwise finished.

Weave in the ends.

Tip: To make puntas for the finished edges, like the neckline and the lower edges of the sleeves, begin as for the cast-on puntas (pages 137 to 139). As your strip of puntas gets longer, hold it up to the opening you will be trimming until it's the correct length. You can either bind off the strip and sew it in place on the garment (this is easiest) or leave the stitches live and either stitch or graft the trim in place.

Bibliography

Bøhn, Annichen Sibbern. *Norwegian Knitting Designs*. Oslo: Grøndahl and Son Publishers, 1975.

Budd, Ann. *The Knitter's Handy Guide to Yarn Requirements*. Loveland, Colorado: Interweave Press, 2004.

Dale Yarn Company. *Knit Your Own Norwegian Sweaters: Complete Instructions for 50 Authentic Sweaters, Hats, Mittens, Gloves, Caps, Etc.* New York: Dover Publications, 1974.

Editors of Vogue Knitting Magazine. *Vogue Knitting*. New York: Pantheon Books, 1989. New edition. New York: Sixth and Spring Books, 2002.

Gibson-Roberts, Priscilla A., and Deborah Robson. *Knitting in the Old Way: Designs and Techniques from Ethnic Sweaters*. Fort Collins, Colorado: Nomad Press, 2004.

Hiatt, Beryl, and Linden Phelps. *Simply Beautiful Sweaters*. Bothell, Washington: Martingale and Company, 1999.

LeCount, Cynthia Gravelle. *Andean Folk Knitting: Traditions and Techniques from Peru and Bolivia*. Saint Paul, Minnesota: Dos Tejedoras Fiber Arts Publications, 1990.

Lewandowski, Marcia. *Andean Folk Knits: Great Designs from Peru, Chile, Argentina, Ecuador and Bolivia*. New York: Lark Books, 2005.

McGregor, Sheila. *The Complete Book of Traditional Scandinavian Knitting*. New York: Saint Martin's Press, 1984.

Square, Vicki. *The Knitter's Companion*. Expanded and updated edition. Loveland, Colorado: Interweave Press, 2006.

Sundbø, Annemor. *Setesdal Sweaters: The History of the Norwegian Lice Pattern*. Kristiansand, Norway: Torridal Tweed, 2001.

Swansen, Meg. *Meg Swansen's Knitting*. Loveland, Colorado: Interweave Press, 1999.

van der Klift-Tellegen, Henriette. *Knitting from the Netherlands: Traditional Dutch Fishermen's Sweaters*. Asheville, North Carolina: Lark Books, 1985.

Index

Chart symbols

FOR TEXTURE PATTERNS

☐   knit (k) on right side, purl (p) on wrong side

⊟   purl (p) on right side, knit (k) on wrong side

FOR COLOR PATTERNS

☐   main color

⊙   contrasting color

Acknowledgments

As every book author must eventually admit, creating a book is a team effort. The author writes the manuscript, and many other people help to turn the text into a book. I'd like to thank the following people for inspiring or contributing to the final results:

Priscilla Gibson-Roberts and Meg Swansen, for the original inspiration.

Debbie O'Neill, for designing and knitting the sweaters on the cover (she tells their stories on pages 121 and 163); Dominic Cotignola, for putting up with my nit-picking during the cover photo shoot; and Monica Thomas, for creating the beautiful cover design.

Helen Marshall, for helping me check the charts by knitting swatches; Kaye Collins, for teaching a fantastic class in which I learned how to knit (or, rather, purl) in the Andean style; and Joanne Turcotte, at Plymouth Yarns, for providing the yarn for the cover sweaters and most of the sample swatches.

Joyce M. Turley, Gayle Ford, and Deborah Robson for creating the illustrations that brought my ideas to life; Kathryn Banks for doing the detail work of copy editing, proofreading, and indexing; and Ann Budd for her technical expertise.

Rebekah Robson-May for all of her help behind the scenes in so many ways that I'll never know.

And special thanks to Deborah Robson, my publisher and editor, for pulling it all together with grace and panache.

Colophon

Text fonts are LTC Goudy Sans (Frederic Goudy and Colin Kahn; Lanston Type Company/ P22), Gill Sans (Eric Gill; Adobe), and Okey Dokey NF (Nick Curtis; Nick's Fonts). Display fonts and dingbats are Abbey Road NF (Nick Curtis; Nick's Fonts), P22 Peanut Pro (Michael Clark; P22), Arrows (The FontSite), Dingbats, FF Dingbests (Johannes Erler and Olaf Stein; FontFont), P22 Tulda (Frau Jenson; P22), LTC Vine Leaves (Lanston Type Company/P22), and Adobe Wood Type Ornaments (Barbara Lind and Joy Redick; Adobe). As noted on the copyright page, the charts were prepared in Knitter's Symbols (David Xenakis; XRX).

Other books you may enjoy

Arctic Lace: Knitting Projects and Stories Inspired by Alaska's Native Knitters

by **Donna Druchunas**

Alaska's Oomingmak Musk-Ox Producers' Co-operative, qiviut, and lace knitting. Winner of a 2007 Independent Publisher Book Award (IPPY) bronze medal and a 2006 ForeWord Book of the Year Award silver medal.

ISBN 978-0-9668289-7-9 (paperback)

Knitting in the Old Way: Designs and Techniques from Ethnic Sweaters

by **Priscilla A. Gibson-Roberts** and **Deborah Robson**

A classic book on traditional and ethnic knitting. Full of ways to apply the skills you've learned here. Finalist in the Independent Publisher Book Award (IPPY), ForeWord Book of the Year Award, and Colorado Book Award competitions and recipient of a *Library Journal* starred review.

ISBN 978-0-9668289-6-2 (paperback), 978-0-9668289-2-4 (Smyth-sewn hardcover)

Spinning in the Old Way: How (and Why) to Make Your Own Yarn with a High-Whorl Handspindle

by **Priscilla A. Gibson-Roberts**

A friendly book on how to spin your own yarn with a portable, inexpensive, efficient tool. Winner of a 2006 ForeWord Book of the Year Award bronze medal.

ISBN 978-0-9668289-8-6 (paperback)

Simple Socks, Plain and Fancy

by **Priscilla A. Gibson-Roberts**

A sock-master's all-time favorite techniques.

ISBN 978-0-9668289-4-1 (paperback)

Available from yarn shops, bookstores, and www.nomad-press.com

Eco-audit

Nomad Press and the printer of this book, Thomson-Shore, both participate in the Green Press Initiative (www.greenpressinitiative.org) and are signatories of the Book Industry Treatise on Reponsible Paper Use.

Nomad Press is committed to preserving ancient forests and natural resources. We elected to print *Ethnic Knitting Discovery* on 50% post consumer recycled paper, processed chlorine free. As a result, for this printing, we have saved:

16 Trees (40' tall and 6-8" diameter)
6,830 Gallons of Wastewater
2,747 Kilowatt Hours of Electricity
753 Pounds of Solid Waste
1,479 Pounds of Greenhouse Gases

Nomad Press made this paper choice because our printer, Thomson-Shore, Inc., is a member of Green Press Initiative, a nonprofit program dedicated to supporting authors, publishers, and suppliers in their efforts to reduce their use of fiber obtained from endangered forests.

For more information, visit www.greenpressinitiative.org